101

Reasons Why

is Better than

ENGLAND

101

Reasons Why

IRELAND

is Better than

ENGLAND

PAT FITZPATRICK

MERCIER PRESS

MERCIER PRESS

Cork

www.mercierpress.ie

© Pat Fitzpatrick, 2020

ISBN: 978 1 78117 768 6

A CIP record for this title is available from the British Library.

Printed and bound in the EU.

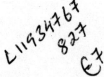

INTRODUCTION

This book is dedicated to Nigel Farage.

If it weren't for him, I'd be arguing that Ireland is better than one of the most progressive and open-minded nations in the world and you'd all think that I was a complete gobshite.

But now we have a new England, which is really an old England, and hardly anyone likes it. So I've only two words for you, Nigel – cheers mate.

SECTION I

WORLD-CLASS TOURIST ATTRACTIONS

I

SKELLIG MICHAEL

A friend comes over from England and you decide to show him something so amazing about Ireland that he heads home feeling absolutely shit about his own country. So you bring him on the boat out to Skellig Michael, off the coast of Kerry, and give him some well-worn chat.

YOU: This is where Irish monks saved western civilisation while ye were still scratching yeer arses in a cave.

HIM: We gave the world Shakespeare, The Beatles and the rule of law. What has this rock got over Cambridge and Oxford?

YOU: You don't have to be rich to come here. And the key texts of Greek and Roman philosophy would have been lost during the carnage of the Dark Ages if the monks on Skellig Michael hadn't written them down for posterity.

HIM: Do you not feel odd boasting about monks, given your history with the Catholic Church?

YOU: You take your wins where you can get them. Are you not impressed that almost 20,000 visitors trek out here every year to pay tribute to this amazing seat of learning?

HIM: Is that why everyone on this boat has a toy Lightsaber?

YOU: One or two might be here because the island featured in *Star Wars*.

HIM: Sorry mate, but are you going to spend the next three days having a go at me because I'm English?

YOU: That's nothing compared to 800 years of oppression.

HIM: What about your 100,000 welcomes?

YOU: Ah, that's just some old shit we roll out for the Yanks.

2

BIG BEN ME BOLLOCKS

It's not that long since people in London were arguing over whether or not they should strike Big Ben on 31 January 2020 to celebrate Brexit, and how much it would cost per bong. It's not clear if the bong in question was the one they were all smoking from – but if I had to guess, I'd say YES.

It's sad to see Big Ben getting dragged into this. He sounds like a nice old fella, with a name suggesting a lovable bear that is just dying for people to get along. Instead, this big old bell has been refuelling the question about England that has puzzled mankind for centuries – how the Jesus did this lot conquer a quarter of the planet?

A far better bell is Shandon Bells in Cork. You can

climb up the bell tower for a fiver and ring out whatever you like, whether it's the theme tune from *Game of Thrones* or maybe 'Hey Jude'. This feature has a touch of celebration about it and even brings people together – especially those living in the warren of streets below the tower, who all agree that it's driving them around the twist. ('Hey Jude' is brilliant the first time you hear it on the bells. After that, not so much.)

Whatever, it's just a bit of fun. Unlike the grim goings-on with poor Big Ben – that was just bongkers. (Sorry.)

3

THE IRISH PUB

Pop quiz. How many times have you met a tourist anywhere in the world looking for directions to the nearest English pub? Never, except maybe an English person on the Costa del Sol complaining that the place is overrun with foreigners.

No, your average tourist wants an Irish pub, of which there are two types. The first is overseas and will often be called 'Irish Pub', because there is no point in complicating these things. It is full of Irish emigrants who swore they would immerse themselves in the local culture, only to discover that Canadians aren't really into drinking. So they huddle around pint bottles of Bulmers, watching a GAA match they're not interested in, because they need something to talk about when they

FaceTime the old man tomorrow.

The second kind of Irish bar is, unsurprisingly, in Ireland. Unlike your English pub, it won't have a name like 'The Bishop's G-String' because that's just silly and drinking is a serious business. A local Irish pub is more likely to be called O'Hanlon's, with a woman called O'Hanlon behind the bar. Nobody ever messes with Mrs O'Hanlon. She's the main reason we love the place.

The other difference between an Irish and English pub is the lack of slot machines. It's a strange one, but Irish people don't like gambling in a pub, unless it's with their liver. (Or someone else's liver; it's never been easier to get a transplant.)

4

NEWGRANGE VS STONEHENGE

The Stone Age passage tomb at Newgrange is 200 years older than England's Stonehenge. Take that, you Johnny-Come-Lately pile of standing stones. (Newgrange is also older than the Great Pyramids of Giza, in case any Egyptian reading this is feeling good about themselves.)

Reportedly, the government in London is planning to build a tunnel near Stonehenge that will wreck precious ancient features, according to conservationists and druids. (I normally steer clear of using druids to support my argument, but needs must.) A lot of English people don't seem to care about this act of vandalism – what's 3,000 years of history compared to shorter journey times on the A303?

We'd never ransack Newgrange like that. It's not because we're arch-conservationists – google 'Wood Quay Viking' or 'Overcrowding at Hill of Tara' if you want to see our record there. Newgrange is precious because, at sunrise during the winter solstice, the ingenious roof-box at the entrance allows light to penetrate all the way into the burial chamber. This corresponds with another ancient annual ritual in Ireland, where we show a video of this happening on the news that night in the hope that some English people will see it and realise 'thick Paddy' is anything but, and actually comes from a long line of brainboxes.

You see, Newgrange adds ten points to our national IQ. We're not going to undermine that with a tunnel.

5

GIANT'S CAUSEWAY

Or the 'What the Fuck Causeway?' as it's known to people who see it for the first time. The Trade Descriptions Act obviously came into force after they named this rocky outcrop on the north Antrim coast. Let's just say the word 'giant' is misleading.

I'm surprised a group of American tourists – 'I thought it would be bigger, Chad' – haven't taken a class action against the Causeway for false advertising. (If you think a certain type of American won't sue a volcanic rock formation, then you need to watch more daytime TV.)

That said, there is a reason the attraction rates 4.5 on TripAdvisor. And that is because it's very, very attractive. An objective Kerry person would probably even concede that this is the most gorgeous stretch of coast on the island – if there were such a thing as an objective Kerry person. (They're more likely to concede that Dingle is on its fourth Fungie.) It certainly beats any stretch of coast in England.

And anyway, size isn't everything (a phrase Chad keeps hearing from his missus) when it comes to rock formations. The weird precision of the hexagons at the Giant's Causeway is as impressive as the legend behind them. Apparently, it was formed when Fionn MacCumhail tossed the rocks into the sea so he could walk across to Scotland and teach some local giant a lesson. However, the Scottish giant ended up chasing him back across the water, meaning that Fionn's wife had to disguise Fionn as a baby to hide him. But when the Scot saw the size of 'the baby', he decided that the dad must be enormous, and so retreated homeward tae think again.

In your face King Arthur's round table – that's what we call a legend over here.

6

A BETTER SECOND CITY

Belfast is the second city of Ireland. Now this will be seen as a provocative statement by a threatened minority on the island who feel that everyone is out to get them. But that's Cork people for you.

Belfast has an undeserved image problem. Every second city has its rundown areas, says anyone who's been to Birmingham. At least Belfast has an excuse. (A thirty-year war, before you ask – I don't want to assume that everyone here has read the same history.) In reality, Belfast is handsome and intriguing and at least half of the people there feel British. (There's something it has in common with Dublin, says anyone from outside The Pale.)

Belfast is perfect for a city break. There's the Crown Bar for a pint, and an award-winning walking tour called

'A History of Terror', which sounds like a lot more fun than plodding around some giant cathedral in Spain because you need a break from the sun. The Titanic Experience is a top museum, particularly if you are tired of celebrating unqualified success stories, because, in fairness, it sank. Outside the city, you're a dash away from some of the most amazing coastline in Europe (see the aforementioned not-so-Giant's Causeway).

This is in contrast to England's second city, Birmingham, which describes itself as the 'Venice of the North' because it has a few canals – and a very, very good sense of humour.

Be careful, though, if you plan to use Belfast as a base for a tour around *Game of Thrones* locations in Northern Ireland. Nothing says 'worst day ever' more than being stuck on a mini-bus full of nerds from Minnesota swapping phrases in Dothraki. So if you do decide to go to The Dark Hedges for Instagram moments, make sure you go on your own.

7

THE CLIFFS

The white cliffs of Dover are the first thing you see as you approach England from the south-east. Thanks to increased erosion, they could soon be the first thing you see of Scotland. But then what else would you expect from a weak-ass, chalky cliff?

You don't get that from the cliffs of Moher, on the west coast of Ireland. They're made of a tough limestone that has been around for 320 million years, which is nearly the amount in euro that you have to pay at the official car park.

Stand on the cliffs of Moher on a clear day (the next one is due in 2023) and you can see awesome sea-stacks, sea-caves and a haunting view of the horizon. Peer out from the cliffs of Dover, meanwhile, and the view is of ferry-loads of people fleeing Britain because they can't be doing with Brexit.

There's just no comparison. A quick look at Trip-Advisor shows that Moher has had 13,800 visits, while Dover weighs in with a chalky-weak 2,700. The Clare cliffs get a 4.5, which would be a 5 if it weren't for the aforementioned cost of parking. It would be nice to think that this could be less than €8 per adult, but that's unlikely given that Irish tourism's new mission statement is: 'We strive to attract a growing number of visitors with our world-class scenery so we can squeeze the fecking pips out of them, lads.' (Not the actual mission statement of Irish tourism, before ye get all lawyered up.)

8

THE BURREN

'There is not enough water to drown a man, wood enough to hang one, or earth enough to bury.' That's the Burren in North Clare according to General Edmund Ludlow, Cromwellian general, 1651. Most English readers won't spot the trigger word in that last sentence – in fact, the history of Anglo-Irish misunderstanding could be summed up with: 'Are you sure we're talking about the same Cromwell?'

Anyway, the Burren. It's an area of north Clare edging onto Galway Bay which looks something like a giant limestone pavement. The first time you see it, you think you've taken a wrong turn and ended up on the moon. This impression won't necessarily change when you bump into a local either, because Clare people can be a bit loony.

The Burren includes Poulnabrone dolmen, one of Ireland's most iconic megalithic monuments. A portal tomb dating back almost 6,000 years, it consists of standing stones with a giant capstone sitting on top of them. Historians believe this monument is the origin of the Irish funeral condolence 'sorry for your troubles' – acknowledging that, on top of your grief, you'll need to drag giant boulders halfway around Galway Bay just to bury the hoor. (I paraphrase, but not much.)

I'm sure there are dolmens in England as well, probably built by Irishmen, because we're mad for the bit of construction. But wherever they are placed, the locations can't compete with the spectacular, eerie setting of the Burren. And if nothing else, General Ludlow, Poulnabrone shows that it is possible to bury someone in the Burren – as long as you put your back into it. (Ah sure look, he was probably tired after all the massacring.)

9

DUBLIN VS LONDON

I was going to call this bit Cork vs London, but I decided to give London a fighting chance. (Buy my other book; it's much funnier than this one.)

In a way, it's impossible to contrast the two cities. One is over-crowded, over-priced and over-confident. And so is the other. But there are a few things that put Dublin on top.

The first is atmospheric pubs. Dublin still has some absolute belters, like Mulligan's, The Long Hall and Toners. No one has ever said, 'Look at all the eejits in there, chatting away to each other when they could be lobbing money into a fruit machine.'

Then you have the transport system. The Tube seems like a good idea, until you spend thirty-seven minutes crushed up against a very angry businessman during a rush-hour delay in Earls Court, him muttering, 'Every fucking morning, every fucking morning', while you lose the will to live. This sort of delay can happen on public transport in Dublin too, but at least there the businessman is saying, 'Ah sure fuck it, it beats being at work.'

As for the social life in London, I'd recommend Instagram and Snapchat for keeping in touch with your friends; trying to arrange a night out with them in real life is so hard you'd nearly need to start organising it before they were born.

Finally, the summer. I'm not sure if you've heard about this, but they've added an extra layer to the seventh circle of hell. It's called 'London when the temperature goes above thirty'. Dublin doesn't have that kind of summer; just a couple of months we set aside for disappointment, starting in July.

10

BLARNEY CASTLE VS WINDSOR

A tour guide in Blarney in the year 2520 AD: 'The story goes that visitors used to willingly pay to climb up that wall to kiss the stone at the top, because they thought it would improve their banter!'

Here's something to consider before you complain that Irish people will try any old shite to attract tourists – a competing back story is that the Blarney stone was in fact the one Moses struck to find water for the Israelites after they escaped from slavery in Egypt. (At least the gift of the gab thing has some sliver of plausibility.)

As it turns out, Queen Elizabeth I invented this gift of the gab thing by accident. She wanted local chiefs of the time to hand over their castles so they could be used as garrisons against rebellious Ulster chieftains. However, Cormac Mór MacCarthy, 16th Earl of Muskerry (aka 'Maccer' to people who didn't have all day), delayed handing over his gaff in Blarney. He kept coming up with flattering distractions to push out the date: 'I love what you've done with your hair, Liz; I'll have that castle for you next week.' Eventually, she had enough, shouting, 'Blarney, Blarney, I will have no more of this Blarney!' (A chant also popular with Yanks who go there on a wet Tuesday in November.)

The castle and its stunning grounds remain popular for a reason – they're a good day out, weather permitting, and a decent lark if you fancy some stone snogging. It certainly beats buttoned-up Windsor Castle, which is basically a tea-towel supermarket with a castle in the middle.

II

RYANAIR

Ryanair carried 139 million passengers in 2018. These people were taken from their beds and driven to a nearby airport, where they were forced onto flights they didn't want to take. They all hated the experience so much that they vowed to never fly with Ryanair again, which is why there is no recorded case of someone using the airline more than once.

You'd swear this was what happened, judging by the way people talk about Ryanair. Or at least the way some people talk about Ryanair – the kind of people who think life owes them a free bag of peanuts.

Ryanair grew from nothing to become one of the largest airlines in Europe with a simple proposition – pay attention and we'll fly you there for less. Their motto should be: *Not For Eejits*. As long as you follow their (not-very-complicated) rules, you can go Dublin to London return for forty quid. (I can remember pre-Ryanair days when it was the equivalent of €600.)

In fairness, they could probably do a bit with their customer service. Sometimes it feels like their brand promise reads, 'Michael O'Leary is going to call to your house and mock you in front of the neighbours.' But if this alters passengers' behaviour enough so that Ryanair can fly me to Pisa for €50, then count me and almost 140 million others in. And before you ask, English airline easyJet flew 96.1 million passengers last year. So the customers have spoken … while on the eighty-minute bus ride from 'Paris' airport into Paris. But then you can't have everything.

12

THE CLIMATE

It happens every summer now – mayhem outside electrical stores across Ireland as people queue to buy a new TV.

The problem is the weather – particularly the front that noses its north-easterly path between Ireland and Britain, hitting land somewhere around south Wales. East of that front it's 'Phwoar What A Scorcher' headlines, as people around London pass out from the heat. West of that front, however, people in Ireland are putting their foot through the telly because we saw the weather forecast on the BBC and want a chance to pass out from the heat as well.

Who cares that a two-day Irish heatwave is enough to have people weeping into their barbecues because we can't sleep with the heat, not to mention the depression that comes after drinking eight bottles of Pinot Grigio in forty-eight hours? We Irish demand our fair share of global warming!

And there's the point. Summers in England are going to get more and more unbearable. That doesn't mean it's going to get any better here – after all, *samhradh* is the Irish word for sitting on damp garden furniture because it stopped raining for half an hour. But at least we won't be panting like dogs in a London apartment because we can't afford an air-conditioner thanks to Brexit. Some of us will wish we were, of course, because part of the Irish condition is to envy people in hot countries. But that doesn't make it right.

13

THE DART

Before it became the DART, the track out from Dublin's Westland Row to Kingstown (now Dún Laoghaire), which opened in 1834, was the first dedicated commuter line of its kind in the world. Take that other countries, including England.

In fairness, Ireland has gone backwards on the commuter rail front since then. The bar fell so low that Dubliners got very excited over two LUAS tram lines in 2004, even though they didn't even intersect. But there is an upside to having the Worst Public Transport System In The World™. At least you know where you stand. There is no need to figure out the nearest DART station to West Dublin, because there isn't one.

This might seem like a bad thing until you decide to

take a short hop on The Tube in London. That's because there is no such thing as a short hop on The Tube in London. In most stations, it's actually a sleight of hand, where you walk ninety-five per cent of the distance to your destination and then get a packed train the rest of the way.

On the other hand, if you need to go from A to B along the coast of Dublin, the DART is one of public transport's great delights. The views out to sea are jaw-dropping, and Posh English visitors will love the way the locals start to sound more and more like them the closer you get to Lansdowne Road.

14

THE RIVER SHANNON

At 360km, this is the longest river in Ireland. The longest river in England is the Severn, at a pitiful 354km, or 220 miles if you still do things the imperial way. (Given their resistance to change, it's amazing that England's currency isn't still Bronze Age arrowheads.)

Anyway, this makes the Shannon the longest river in a place that you definitely can't call the British Isles. We've tried a few alternatives to the British Isles. You'll hear them referred to as 'these islands', which sounds weirdly like something Jacob Rees-Mogg would say, and therefore completely wrong. West Europe Archipelago is out because archipelago sounds like a guy who played for Aberdeen in the 1980s. The Anglo-Celtic Isles sounds like a 1970s song contest that died out due to popular demand. British-Irish Isles is really hard to say with a few pints in you, which is a shame, because it's exactly the sort of thing you'd say in a pub, just before the barman says, 'Alright lads, we'll have none of that in here.'

Hopefully this will get sorted out soon. One suggestion, given Brexit tensions, is that Ireland and Scotland should agree to call them Oileáin Michael Collins William Wallace, just to get a little dig in on the English. I can't believe it hasn't been considered.

Anyway, back to the rivers. The Severn flows through Bristol, which gave the world Banksy, Hannah Murray and Massive Attack. Kudos there, but the Shannon flows into the sea at Limerick, which gave the world Blindboy, Dolores O'Riordan, Kevin Barry and Jimmy Carr's parents. (I was stretching a bit there at the end.)

15

HEDGES

The first thing an English person will notice while driving around the Irish countryside is that some roads are better than others. Where your Englisher is accustomed to smooth surfaces and freshly painted lines, your Irisher knows to bring a flask and sleeping bag in case his car falls into a pothole. This is because we prefer to spend money on new cars over new roads – we're a bit flashy that way.

The second thing you notice driving along country roads in Ireland is the view. There isn't one. Why? Hedgerows.

We decided to leave ours largely intact in order to maintain the rich biodiversity of our countryside. Or maybe we were just lazy – honestly, you can't rule that out. Whatever the reason, Ireland has maintained a higgledy-piggledy countryside compared to England's, where a hedge sparrow can feck right off if it thinks it's going to stop the efficient use of combine harvesters.

You might argue that the hedges in Ireland mean you can't see that much when you're driving around. But trust me, once you've seen one field, you've seen them all. And the beauty of a high hedge is that there is a surprise around every corner – even if it's just a short stretch of fresh tarmac and a few road markings. (And posters from four different county councillors saying, 'I did this! Go on, give us a vote.')

SECTION 2

LOCAL CUSTOMS & MORE

16

THE IRISH FUNERAL

Over in England, you have to wait a few weeks after someone dies before you can bury them. That must be very hard on their loved ones – you'd be massive from all the ham sandwiches.

We like to get things done quicker over here, in case the property market turns and the proceeds from Mammy's house can no longer fund your villa in Sardinia. (That's when the real grieving starts.)

Irish funerals are full of laughter; we get very giddy when we're setting out on three days of solid drinking. Only messing – thanks to the whole wellness boom, these days most people try to keep it down to two.

There are a number of stock phrases associated with the Irish funeral. The first one is, 'You'll come back to the house.' This often has a silent 'over my dead body' at the end, because you've invited 200 people already and you know the way Uncle Christy gets bonkers from the gin.

Another example is a stock phrase that takes all the stress out of going to an Irish funeral. There's no need to worry about what you should say to relatives of the deceased; just grab every hand in the front row of the funeral home and say, 'Sorry for your troubles.' (Unless of course the funeral is in Northern Ireland, because people might think it's a strange time to bring up politics.)

Other popular phrases at an Irish funeral include 'Of course he was a complete bollocks' and 'Any sign of the will?' People think these phrases rather than saying them, though – at least until the whiskey comes out.

17

A STRONG CONSTITUTION

Sorry for the public house language, but the Irish Constitution is a pain in the hole. The 1937 version, Bunreacht na hÉireann, must have been communicated in a fever-dream to Éamon de Valera by an angel dressed as the archbishop of Dublin. (Have you got a better explanation?) If you had to summarise that constitution in one sentence it would read: Get back in the kitchen, woman. It took us forty years to overhaul the thing so that it didn't look like a hate crime against gays and Protestants.

But at least it served a purpose. At the time of writing, England is still part of something called the United Kingdom. By the time you read this, though, it could be like North Korea, or maybe a dystopian cartoon on Netflix. A lot of this recent chaos came about because they never bothered to write down their own constitution. As a result, I'm not sure how the country is supposed to work. Reading between the lines, I think the Queen owns the place, really, but she isn't allowed to sell it.

The only person who knows how it all hangs together is some duffer in a tweed suit called Sir Bunty King-Lickington, QC, OBE. Don't worry about Bunty's qualifications, though; the important thing is that he went to Eton.

I feel for the English on this one, really – no one writes stuff down any more. But they've made huge strides in transcription software now, so come on, all you have to do is ask Bunty to do a brain dump. It could prevent so many issues in the future – particularly if you can somehow manage to find an app that understands Bunty's accent.

18

THE METRIC SYSTEM

Look England, it's not that you still talk about pounds and ounces. It's more the way you abbreviate pounds as 'lbs'. What's the story there? Would it have killed you to make it 'pds'. Or just use pounds; I mean, it's not even a long word, really.

No one here misses the imperial system. (For any English reader wondering why we might have a problem with imperial measurement, the clue is in the name.) For starters, there are 1,760 yards in a mile. This isn't because 1,760 is an easy number to work with, because it really isn't. It's something to do with a mile being the distance a Roman soldier covered in 1,000 paces. Fair play to the English for holding on to a measurement system based on Italian walking habits – and there was I thinking they hated Europeans.

Here's our guilty secret, though. Any Irish person born before 1990 still thinks in miles, which we convert into kilometres in our heads in case people think we're old. As a result, no other country can lay a hand on us when it comes to multiplying by 0.621371 on the fly. If only it were a sport in the Olympics.

Of course there is one other unit of imperial measurement we'll always hold on to. Pints. We'll cling on to those with our cold, grey hands – literally, in a lot of cases.

19

THE IRISH PASSPORT

It's hard to imagine anyone swapping their Irish passport these days for a blue one with a crown on the front. The swapping is all in the other direction now, as people scramble to avoid sharing a nationality with Jacob Rees-Mogg. (A very wise choice, madam, as he might say himself.)

But then an Irish passport has always been hot property. This is partially down to our principled stance on neutrality since independence (aka we were too corrupt half the time to afford a proper army). And also, when Irish people were involved in colonising a quarter of the planet, we did it in a red coat and so our neighbours took the blame. We should probably acknowledge that as well.

As a result, a passport with a harp on the front is welcome at border posts all over the world, even the Middle East. It probably explains why the CIA decided to use fake Irish passports during the Iran–Contra affair in the 1980s, the most famous going to Lieutenant Colonel Oliver North. (Look it up if you haven't heard of the whole affair; the Yanks were well dodgy.)

Being associated with that mightn't look great now, but you must remember that Ireland was so short of confidence in the 1980s that the country came to a standstill if we won a prize at showjumping. So our first reaction when the Iran–Contra scandal broke was 'They chose us!', followed by 'Isn't that colonel very handsome in his uniform?'

We're much more grown-up and assured now. In fact, we'd be appalled to hear that someone has gotten their hands on a dodgy Irish passport, unless they have a net worth of over 10 million dollars. (Interested? Our agents are standing by, waiting for your call, so phone

1-800-WeWouldSellOurShaggingGranny right now and claim your free shillelagh. And don't forget that we have a special scrappage deal for Saudi princes looking to trade in their UK passport.)

20

THE FINGER

How do you know when you've crossed from urban to rural Ireland? Someone gives you 'the finger'.

This isn't the road-rage middle finger that people prefer in England – it's a beautifully slow lift of the index finger off the steering wheel. The first time you see it, you think: did that just happen? Then the next driver does it, and the one after that.

It's a little celebration of rural life – it's a 'Isn't it lucky we have the time and inclination to acknowledge a stranger passing by?' If you're ever feeling a bit down, try a trip along a country road; all those finger-hugs could be just the lift you need.

Soon you're finger lifting with the best of them. Your technique won't be right the first time, in the same way that a newbie can't sit down at a piano and bash out a bit of Mozart. There might be a little bit of soreness after the first few trips, particularly if you're in Kerry. (The finger lift is compulsory down there, even on main roads.) But the little rush of belonging is well worth it.

Then, without warning, an oncoming driver fails to reciprocate your finger wave. The bastard. What's his story now, you ask, before you see the 50km/hr sign ahead down the road. And you're heading back into town.

21

GIVE US A SIGN

The first thing you notice when you arrive in England is sign after sign telling you what to do. (They probably have a sign in Heathrow telling you to keep an eye out for them.)

You get on the Tube and there is an announcement telling you how to use the escalator, followed by a statistic telling you how many people are injured every year because they don't use the handrail. This is a sly dig at people visiting from Ireland who underestimate the strength of real ale.

If you do see a sign in Ireland, it's along the lines of 'If anything bad happens here now, lads, it's yeer own fault.' (If you're wondering why this is the case, try to get a quote for public liability insurance.)

This light-touch signage is particularly true when you come across a diversion in Ireland. There you are, driving down a narrow country road, when an orange diversion sign directs you down an even narrower road. At the next crossroads, another orange sign helps you on your way, same thing at the crossroads after that. And then … nothing. There are conflicting explanations for the lack of direction at the fourth crossroads, but let's face it, they ran out of signs.

The bad news is you are now officially lost. The good news is you are officially lost in the Irish countryside. So sit back, enjoy and don't forget the finger wave.

22

HALLOWEEN

It's an Irish thing, based on the Celtic festival of *Samhain*, another word carefully designed so it can only be pronounced by the People of the Freckles. (Go with sow-win.)

It is said to have started on the Hill of Ward in Meath, where a great fire was lit at the halfway point between the autumn equinox and winter solstice. This grew into a thing over time, until the Yanks got their hands on it and turned it into a sweet-eating competition.

It turns out our Celtic ancestors believed that the barrier between the real and spirit world was thin at this time, which meant that your dead grandmother could come back and catch you masturbating. (No wonder we're weird about sex.) The problem with this thin barrier was that it also allowed for an influx of 'the little people'. This phrase has a different meaning in England, where it's the term the Royal Family uses to describe people who pay into Buckingham Palace. In Ireland, it was a reference to evil spirits with height issues.

People used to blacken their faces during *Samhain*, to make them look dead and therefore safe from these little people. This led to the modern-day custom for wearing hideous clothes on 31 October. Or, in Ireland's case, the entire 1980s. (We've seen that photo of you wearing a skinny leather tie – what were you thinking?)

23

SHOPS

There isn't much difference between the High Street in England and Ireland. Other than the fact that there is no such place as a High Street in Ireland, because people would accuse you of thinking you are above them. (We're more a Low Street kind of vibe.) That said, the 'High Street' shops on our big streets are pretty much the same as those in England.

However, when it comes to the smaller shops where you get your 'few bits', Ireland is the clear winner. This is mainly down to the shopkeepers.

There are two types of people behind the counter at a small shop in England. The first is polite but distant. There will be a lot of 'sir' and 'madam', but not a lot of fun. This is much better than the second type, though, who has been on a two-day customer experience course in a Ramada hotel near the M4 and wants to know if you have anything exciting planned for the afternoon, which is unlikely, because you're in Rochdale.

The Irish shopkeeper, in contrast, doesn't give a shit about your overall experience – they just want to be loved. This goes to the heart of what it means to be Irish. They are so terrified that you won't like them that they can't even ask for payment without adding on the phrase 'when you're ready': '€3.30, when you're ready,' they say, because it isn't nice to rush people.

A note here for visitors: don't take the money out of your wallet, put it back in again and say, 'I'm not ready yet.' Smartarse isn't really our sense of humour and we can get fierce cranky in a queue.

24

PACK OF RIDES

I'm not suggesting that the Irish are a good-looking race in general. Five minutes sitting next to a Dutch family on holidays is enough to make us glad that we have a great personality. (How come they have such good tans? It's always lashing in Amsterdam.)

The point here is that when Irish people are good-looking, they are any-chance-of-a-shag good-looking. This goes back to Maureen O'Hara, who showed that you could do some very interesting things with red hair. Now we have Ruth Negga, Aisling Bea, Sarah Greene and, of course, Saoirse Ronan, who isn't immediately good-looking – which is the best kind.

The men's team includes Roy Keane, Cillian Murphy, Gabriel Byrne, Liam Neeson, Jamie Dornan, Colin

Farrell and Aidan Turner's chest. The only English actors who belong in this company are Jeremy Irons and Dominic West, which is probably why they both moved to Ireland to live in a castle. (Separate castles, before you ask, but it would make a great idea for a sitcom: Dominic starts a laundry business in the west wing called 'Jeremy Irons'. It needs a bit of work; leave it with me.)

Where were we? Oh yeah, looks. We've got stunners in all shapes and sizes and colours. And they said there was no upside to thousands of years of colonisation, invasion and oppression. The big eejits.

25

THE ACCENT

What else can you say about the Irish accent, except that there isn't just one. This can come as a surprise to American visitors, when the woman at passport control doesn't greet them with, 'Is it the way you might be visitin' the old country, shillelagh Bono potatoes?'

We have an incredible array of accents. Your average Cork accent is what happens when you give helium to a Welsh hummingbird who has relations in Pakistan. Meanwhile, the working-class Dublin accent is an attempt at the world record for long vowels, while the posh one sounds like you have a medical condition. The midlands and border accents are bordering on plain weird, like having breakfast with a walrus. And then there's sexy Donegal. A generation of Irish men had to live with the fact that every time Shay Given spoke on TV, their partner considered leaving them.

No English accent can come close. To be fair, I can't offer an objective view of an upper-class English accent, because when we hear one we immediately think of the famine. It's like how every time Jacob Rees-Mogg said 'our friends in Orland' during the Brexit negotiations we added another century onto the 800 years of oppression. These things can't be helped.

In the non-posh category, Cockneys always sound as if they're late and angry. Similarly, it doesn't matter what you say in a Manchester accent, it sounds like a complaint. People in Yorkshire seem much happier with their lives, although it's hard to see why. People from the north-east, meanwhile, will always struggle to be taken seriously because of *Geordie Shore*. As for Birmingham, don't go there. (No one else does – why should you?)

26

EMIGRATION

To be clear, not everything about Irish emigration is good. The songs are diabolical, for one thing – it's basically 'I'm Far Away From', followed by the name of your local parish, or your mammy. Other than that, though, emigration has been fairly amazing for Ireland. Okay, Mam is upset because her kids are in Sydney and Da is upset because Mam is upset and he keeps getting killed for everything. (Or 'kilt' as it's pronounced locally). But Mam's children don't really care – they're basically shagging a hot foreigner on Bondi Beach. (Relax, Mam, it's a figure of speech.)

England is different. They don't seem to have our culture of travelling en masse to another country, unless it's as part of an invasion force. As a result, you get people left stewing in towns that have seen better days, blaming it all on Johnny Foreigner.

There was no shortage of documentaries during Brexit showing the sad decline of post-industrial towns in England. Irish people have the same reaction to every single one of them – 'What are you still doing living in that shit town, you big eejit!!?'

If this were Ireland, there would be a sign at the entrance to the town saying, 'Every last one of us is in Australia shagging a stranger on the beach; give us a shout if things improve.' (Again, Mam, it's just a figure of speech. They're probably shagging someone from back home.)

27

THE MULTINATIONALS

There are still some people in Ireland who think we'd be better off without the multinationals. You can actually hear the wind blowing around in their heads. Bear in mind that there was a time when the main occupation in Ireland was waving at coachloads of American tourists. That changed the minute we started giving American businesses the eye.

They came here and found that, contrary to the stereotype of us being lazy drunks, we were actually very hard-working drunks. (This is down to the J1 experience, where a generation of Irish students spent a summer in the States and found they had to work forty jobs to be able to afford the rent on a studio apartment in Cape Cod that they shared with twenty-three lads from Tipperary.)

The result was that Ireland went from the 'Poor Man of Europe' to 'Have you seen my new sunglasses, bitch?' (We're new to wealth, give us time.) Now we have the second highest GDP per capita in the EU, compared to the UK down at 10. (And that's when they were still in the EU.)

In fairness, we know that Britain is about to take a great leap forward, because Boris Johnson said so. It's hard to see which industries are about to take off, but if I had any money, I'd be putting it into companies that make time machines big enough to bring entire countries back to 1945.

28

THE CLASS SYSTEM

The upper class in Ireland is known as 'Shane Ross'. He was once the minister for transport, tourism and sport. During his tenure as minister he had an address at the Arrivals Hall in Dublin Airport, so he could get in a photo with any returning Irish athlete who won something. Shane is so posh that we are not allowed to make eye contact with him – he's basically a Sun God with an Irish scarf.

The next layer of society down from him is Leinster Schools Rugby, where steroid giants called Turlough speak to each other in American accents. You have to be born into this level, no exceptions (unless your name is Tadhg Furlong).

Below that is a thin layer of people who got rich

during the Celtic Tiger years and set about ruining Ireland's reputation for modesty and intelligence, usually with a pair of expensive sunglasses on their heads. You can get into this level if you like, but you really don't want to.

The other ninety-nine per cent of the population is middle Ireland or working class, depending on whether you'd choose rugby over darts.

The best thing about our pecking order? Deference. There isn't any. Unlike in England, where people admire posh types because their ancestors were good at stealing land during the Middle Ages. We tried that kind of deference here with the bishops and it didn't work out for us at all. So now we have a new mode of social organisation – everyone looks down on everyone else. It really suits our personality.

29

FAIR PLAY

The English are famous for their sense of fair play among countries that weren't colonised by them. Sorry old chap, but it's hard to see past all the slaughtering, land grabs and famine. Just ask anyone in India – being a good sport on the cricket pitch is never going to make up for the Amritsar Massacre. (Even if the lieutenant-governor at the time was actually from Tipperary. Say nothing.)

In fairness, the English are not even pretending to be fair any more. Up until ten years ago, football pundits would go crazy if Johnny Foreigner threw himself over in the box to get a penalty. Now they're pretty much saying 'nice dive' if Johnny Englishman does it. (While reminding us all that he caught this snakiness from Johnny Foreigner, who can't be trusted.)

As for gaining an unfair advantage, let's just say a lot of English athletes seem to have problems with nasal congestion coming up to a major event. (Google 'marginal gains' there if you fancy a laugh.)

Now, no one is suggesting the Irish play fair. To be honest, we're dodgy as fuck half the time. But we have our own version of fair play – it's where someone you thought was dodgy does something decent and you say, 'Fair play to them.' It's honest and sincere, which is more than you can say for the fair play they like to bang on about across the water.

30

THE ANGELUS

A catch-up for any foreign readers: we pause at 12 p.m. and 6 p.m. every day in Ireland to say, 'What the fuck? Is that the Angelus? I could have sworn we voted it out in a referendum – how the Jaysus is that still going on?'

The truth is that Jaysus is going on – or his mother, to be more precise. The pause is on the national broadcaster, RTÉ, where they play the chimes of church bells at these times and we're all supposed to pray to the Virgin Mary, but we don't do it any more because we're so over the Catholic Church.

Still, it seems that we will always have the Angelus with us, a bit like fake tan. It's been updated recently for a more contemporary feel, so instead of Catholic overtones, you have clips of people looking really miserable. This is still fairly religious, though, because it reminds us what we felt like at Mass.

Weirdly, a 2018 poll revealed that sixty-eight per cent of people here want to keep the Angelus on RTÉ. Or maybe it's not so weird. The Catholic Church isn't all bad after all – far from it – and neither is stopping whatever it is you're doing for a bit of reflection. Also, every country holds on to stuff that is well past its sell-by date – just look at the Royal Family. Or *Emmerdale*.

31

FECK, SHITE, JAYSUS

My grandmother couldn't take Jesus Christ's name in vain because she was a very religious woman. So she said, 'Jaysoo Crewsht.' Not a sin.

She was just carrying on the great Irish tradition of curse clones – where we use sound-a-likes because it's not a great look to be cursing your fucking hole off all the time. They don't seem that into it in England, where it's full-on cursing as far as I can see, particularly if you're posh.

Curse cloning isn't just popular because we're trying to stay out of hell. Irish people also want to be correct. Some situations don't call for fuck – it's just too serious, and it makes you look angry and out of control. This is where 'feck' comes in – it's the skimmed milk of F words.

Say your partner forgets to turn on the dishwasher overnight and now the kids' lunch boxes aren't clean. Muttering 'For fuck's sake' here is not a great look – 'for feck sake' is what you want; it makes the point without making you look insane. It also allows you to keep 'for fuck's sake' for the important things, like when Priti Patel appears on the telly.

Another great Irish curse clone is 'shite'. It's basically shit, but with a lovely long 'i' for extra emphasis.

A quick word on 'gobshite'. It's the Irish word for someone who literally talks shit. I can't tell you what it translates to in English, because the lawyers told me to stop picking on Piers Morgan.

32

NUMBER PLATES

It's impossible for an Irish person to drive on English roads. There doesn't seem to be any way to judge other drivers' wealth from the weird jumble of letters and numbers on their number plates – how do people live like this?

When you finally do spot a car from the Irish Republic, your first thought is, 'I wonder do I know them?' The second is to judge them by the value of their car. Anything older than five years and it's clear that life has passed them by. Anything newer than two years, however, and they're taking the piss – or maybe their aunt died and left them a bit of money.

Of course, there is one kind of number plate that seems very at home on an English motorway, and that's a personalised one. We don't allow them in Ireland because no one wants to look like a C0mp13t3 L053R or T0ta1 T0553r.

Saying that, it's not unheard of for an Irish person to go to England and temporarily lose the run of themselves. When Roy Keane arrived at Manchester United, it's said that he started driving around in a large Mercedes with 'Roy 1' on the number plate. The good news is that the plate lasted as long as it took for someone to visit from Cork and reacquaint him with the phrase, 'You're some langer.'

33

THE IRISH WEDDING

A pissed priest, the smell of fake tan, people in awful clothes congratulating each other on their fashion sense, and feverish praying from people who haven't seen the inside of a church in fifteen years – we might never know why a day at the races is exactly the same as an Irish wedding, but that's just the way it is.

Nothing is left to chance for the big day. The mother of the bride puts a headless Child of Prague outside her door the night before, because who doesn't want a decapitated infant at the centre of the happiest day of their lives? Okay, it's actually put out to guarantee a dry day for the wedding. No news yet on why people don't put them out the other 364 nights of the year – it's not as if we're in the middle of a five-year drought over here.

At the heart of the Irish wedding is what we like to call 'The Great Conundrum'. This is where everyone swears the wedding day was the best day of all time and then swears they preferred the barbecue in the local the day after. We've got some very good people working on this conundrum as I write – the best they have come up with so far is to point out that Irish people are liable to say any old shite when there is drink involved.

And then there's the gambling. You're not legally married in Ireland if every table doesn't have a jackpot on speech length, because you'd need something to keep you engaged during the best man's rambling story about some drinking game in Montauk.

We certainly do a better wedding than England, where they rarely get to experience the joy of walking out of the church under an arch of hurleys from the groom's local GAA club.

34

WE'RE SORRY

With tidy gardens, clean cars and world-class queues, it's clear that the English care about etiquette and doing the right thing – although not enough to stop them selling arms to dodgy dictatorships in the Middle East. Who cares about missiles as long as everyone agrees on the correct way to address a minor Royal?

This is because the shameless English lack our old friend 'The Mortification'. Every Irish person comes with this pre-installed. It's why we use the word 'sorry' to get someone's attention. 'Sorry! Sorry! I just wanted to get your attention there so I could apologise for some minor insult you probably didn't notice, but I don't want to take any chances, so sorry, and while I'm at it, I am totally scarlet that it took me so long to come to the point, so sorry for that as well.'

The reason for this non-stop apologising is simple. You don't get respect in Ireland for being a duke, earl or billionaire. You earn respect by being 'sound', or maybe even 'sound out' in cases of extreme soundness. Anything that threatens your status as sound can only be warded off with a flurry of 'sorry, sorry, sorry'. It can be irritating at times, but at least The Mortification has stopped us from selling missiles to dodgy dictators. That would be a very unsound thing to do.

SECTION 3

FAMOUS PEOPLE

35

LUKE 'MING' FLANAGAN

There are two types of colourful politicians in Ireland. One has a Wikipedia page that includes references to things like brown envelopes, tribunals, catchy election tunes and 'attempted to reintroduce drink-driving into rural Ireland'.

The other type is Luke 'Ming' Flanagan, the MEP for Midlands North-West. The only thing he has in common with former English MEP Nigel Farage is that both of them are delighted that Nigel is finally out of the European parliament.

We better start with the Ming bit. According to his website, the nickname comes from a more colourful time in his life when he was known as 'Ming the Merciless'. A bit of a hint there that you're not in Kansas any more.

He revealed in an *Irish Times'* interview that the

name was cemented at a party in his house, where he decided to have one policy in politics – unless Ming the Merciless was elected, Flash Gordon was going to get it. I'm not sure what that means either. And I won't speculate what might have been going on at that party, but Ming is synonymous with the campaign to legalise cannabis. I'll just leave that there with you.

At this point you might think that Ming is one of those sad eccentrics who runs for the Monster Raving Loony Party. Wrong. Just ask the 'serious' politicians he has defeated in elections down the years. Ming is the real deal, an independent voice with a record on speaking out on everything from Irish neutrality to the EU Copyright Directive and the protection of peatlands in his native constituency.

Ming gets a regular kicking from the bigger parties, so he's obviously doing something right. And, come on, there is no way an electorate would elect a clown over and over again – unless he went to Eton, of course.

36

PRINCE ANDREW

I don't want to single out Andy for a hard shoulder in this book, in case he sells his share of London and hires the trickiest lawyer in the world. On the other hand, he's kind of singled himself out. Sometimes it feels like he was put on earth to deliver future plotlines for *The Crown*. Seriously, if aliens ever wanted to strike a killer blow on Planet Earth, all they would have to do is google 'Prince Andrew Scandal' and the Internet will explode. I for one would welcome our alien overlords post-explosion if it meant that Britain could be free from the yoke of our friends in Buckingham Palace, Windsor, Sandringham and Kensington but definitely not Sunderland or Milton Keynes.

The only good thing about the Royals from an Irish

perspective is that we get to ogle their antics without having to doff our cap when they pass by in a giant gold carriage.

And it doesn't look like our neighbours will free themselves from the old cap-doffing any time soon. When a minor royal gets into trouble, they usually get photographed in public with their mammy. (Oi, look, he's with the Queen, he must be alright then.) If that doesn't work, he gets half of Warwickshire. Meanwhile, if the president of Ireland's child brought the country into disrepute, we'd vote that president out, because we can. It's called republicanism and we'd highly recommend it.

37

BLINDBOY

Copying the best is always a good idea, unless you want to be unique. Anyway, enough of the motivational posts I stole from Instagram.

Blindboy and his band, The Rubberbandits, didn't copy anyone. They wore plastic bags on their head and blew holes in the notion that you'll never get anywhere with a raw Limerick accent. (This has been devastating for Cork people, blowing away a lot of the satisfaction we got from *The Young Offenders*.) They rhymed Fitzy with Mitzy in a song about a right rough-looking wedding.

Some say the plastic bags made them look surreal. Others say if you're going to make a video that takes the piss out of people in Limerick, then wearing a plastic bag on your head is a great way to keep your life assurance premium under €8,000.

Blindboy has since turned to podcasting. Listeners all over the world are hooked as he gives his latest hot take on mental health issues, sociology and global capitalism. It's like a TED talk, except he's taken out the patronising tone and replaced it with the c*nt word. What a result. I've just listened to an episode where he is trying to find a quiet spot in a park in Spain. Thanks to his weird genius, it's infinitely more interesting than it sounds.

If England has anything to compete with Blindboy, they're keeping it nice and quiet. (Unlike the Spaniards in the park. Give the podcast a listen and you'll see what I mean.)

38

ST PATRICK VS
ST GEORGE

England's patron saint, St George, was a high-ranking Roman officer who was killed around AD 300. There is no evidence that he ever visited England. Some say putting your trust in foreigners is most un-English. Others would point to the Royal Family, half the English rugby team and Graham Norton.

And yes, I know St Patrick was Welsh originally. But sure they're basically Irish with a couple of 'Ls' at the start. And St Patrick came to Ireland twice – first when he was kidnapped in Wales and delivered into a life of slavery in Co. Antrim. He escaped and headed back home, where, according to his *Confessions*, he heard the voice of the Irish people begging him to come and walk among them again. (If someone said that now, he'd be sent for psychological assessment, but those were different times, so we made him a saint.)

Anyway, the voices persuaded him to come back. Fair play to him for not assuming that it was a trap because we were running low on slaves.

We got on famously after that. So famously that he became our patron saint and St Patrick's Day has become a by-word for good-natured partying all over the world, up until 7 p.m. when the young people emerge from their pre-loading parties and start puking in each other's mouths. Make sure you are out of town by then.

39

GRAHAM NORTON

There is only one response to people who criticise Graham for changing his accent – send them to his hometown of Bandon. A West Cork accent is a thing of beauty right up to the moment you have to interview Salma Hayek in front of millions of viewers on the BBC. After that it's just her going, 'Sorry, did you say something there or was that your impersonation of a tractor on a cold morning?'

Graham is such a pro. It can't be easy listening to a Hollywood superstar banging on about their latest Marvel movie without saying, 'Jesus, stop, we all know you did it for the money.'

Graham is also unpredictable. It isn't every Irishman who would take on the job of agony aunt with *The Daily*

Telegraph. Let's just say it wouldn't be a surprise if Graham got a letter that read, 'Dear Sir, I am worried about all the filthy Micks coming over here and taking our jobs in the media. Colonel Bloody-Foreigners, Maidenhead'.

Maybe he did – Graham quit the *Telegraph* in 2019 because he felt it had gone extra toxic during the Brexit campaign. (I'm on safe ground firing shit at the *Telegraph* – they're about as likely to give this book a positive review as they are to support compulsory sex changes for retired colonels in Maidenhead.)

I doubt Graham misses the agony aunt gig, because he has all the fun jobs sewn up – presenting his own show, covering the Eurovision and hosting an annual table quiz in a tin shed on a peninsula in West Cork.

He's earned the right to do whatever he wants. He isn't just the best host in England – he's the best in the world.

40

JOHN PHILIP HOLLAND

We don't just produce alcoholic writers and rock stars with a Jesus complex. Irish people can invent stuff as well. Holland, from Co. Clare, developed the first submarine for the Royal Navy, HMS *Holland 1*, along with the first one commissioned by the US Navy.

John didn't take to the inventing straightaway. He actually joined the Christian Brothers and was posted to the North Monastery in Cork during the 1850s, where he met another scientifically minded Brother who supported his work. He then decided to leave the Brothers and head to Boston, where he worked on his prototype submarine and found common cause with Irish nationalists. He planned to build a submarine for use against the Royal Navy, but these plans ran aground (sorry) following a rift among the Fenians. There is only one thing Irish people can always agree on – we love a rift.

Holland continued on, anyway, eventually developing a sub for the Royal Navy (the dirty turncoat). The British authorities didn't want to use it in battle originally because they thought it was too sly. Rear Admiral Wilson described it as 'underhand, unfair and damned un-English'. Now there's a man with a sense of humour. They got over this eventually and submarines were a key factor in the First World War.

Holland dreamed that such a lethal weapon would give people pause before going to war. Let's just say, that didn't work out. But with rising sea levels, we might all be driving a sub soon. So here's to the man who might have just ended up saving humanity.

41

TWO MARYS, ONE MARGARET

When Mary Robinson was elected president of Ireland in 1990, Old Ireland jumped into the grave and then turned in it. Because, as the new president said in her acceptance speech, Mná na hÉireann went from rocking the cradle to rocking the system. After all, it wasn't just any woman who had become the first woman to occupy a senior position in Ireland; it was a woman who had fought against injustice as she saw it, even resigning as whip for the Labour Party in 1985 because she felt the Anglo-Irish Agreement overlooked the objections of unionists in Northern Ireland.

When Robinson left – to take up the role of UN High Commissioner for Human Rights – she was replaced by Mary McAleese. You wouldn't mess with Mary McAleese. According to her memoirs, Pope John Paul II tried it when they met, shaking her husband's hand rather than hers and asking him if he'd like to be president rather than his wife. Nice bit of reading the room there from the pope. Mary told him to cop on, saying that she was the elected president of Ireland whether he liked it or not.

In fairness to Margaret Thatcher, she didn't take any crap either. She was happy to destroy anything that got in her way, whether it was a pompous EU official or large swathes of northern England. And she lit up the 1980s by setting the stage for a raft of Tory sex scandals. (When you add them all up, you're looking at nearly as many sex scandals as Boris Johnson has had. Now that's randy.)

You could say Ireland wins here on integrity alone. Or play the numbers game and say that in recent times, Ireland has had two mighty female leaders to England's one. Unless you want to include Theresa May. Which you don't.

42

SAINT BRENDAN

Forget about Christopher Columbus or those killjoy English pilgrims on the *Mayflower* – Ireland's Saint Brendan was the first European to arrive in America.

Of course an Irish person would never say that Saint Brendan 'discovered' America. We're more inclined to point out that the Native Americans got there first, until a greedy horde arrived from the east and said, 'We'll have a bit of that.' We've all been there.

But we do like the story of Brendan, as told in *Navigatio Sancti Brendani Abbatis*, a medieval bestseller (which means it sold five copies). The book says that Brendan set off from sixth-century Kerry and sailed across the Atlantic in a currach, which is basically a large banana covered in leather.

The first thing that appeals about this story is that Brendan is said to have taken on this voyage at the age of ninety-three. Two words for that – hardy man. On the other hand, maybe he weighed up the situation and said, 'What's the worst thing that could happen?'

The second thing to love here is that, unlike the kind of guests who stay for 800 years, Brendan left America after forty days, on the advice of an angel. Note that Brendan didn't enslave half the population and take all their gold. We also like that. Brendan was sound enough to realise that's a shit thing to do to people you've just met. Which is why Brendan is a saint. And Christopher Columbus was just some guy who got lost on his way to India.

43

DERMOT BANNON

Is anyone surprised that our top celebrity professional is a celebrity architect? England likes their celebrity chefs and bakers, because food is a top way to separate yourself from the lower orders. (It's all about class, mate.)

Over here, we do that with property. Man, we love the stuff. Irish people would gladly go without food in order to get their hands on a decent place to live. In fact, that's what 300,000 people under thirty-five are doing in Ireland right now.

Dermot Bannon is the leader of our property cult. He led us out of the darkness, literally, by knocking the wall through to the living room and putting a glass box out the back. He put an end to 'the good room', which was traditionally set aside for parish-priest visits and teenage phone sex with your first girlfriend (hopefully not at the same time).

Let's face it: Bannon is bolshie. On Channel 4's *Place in the Sun*, when Gary and Tracy from Bolton choose the tiny apartment in the old town rather than the spacious villa in the new development full of ex-pats because they'd like to be near the local fish restaurants, the presenter just sits there and says nothing, because English people are very polite.

Bannon doesn't do polite. If Gary and Tracy tried that shit with him, he'd tell them they hate fish almost as much as they hate foreigners, and frogmarch them to the estate agent to buy one of the new villas. He'd probably persuade them to go with a glass box extension out the back as well, even though they were dead set against it at the start.

44

WILLIAM MELVILLE

Three things about William Melville.

1. He was one of the first intelligence agents in MI5.
2. He was from Sneem in south Kerry.
3. Given the number of republicans from that part of the country, it's fair to say that early MI5 wasn't that keen on background checks.

That said, Kerry people make for great spies. For one thing, Melville could have taught early recruits the ancient Kerry art of answering a question with a question. 'Why were you sitting in the park wearing a red carnation and carrying a copy of yesterday's *Daily Express*?' 'Who told you that?'

When he entered the intelligence world he was given the alias 'William Morgan', which was shortened to M. No wonder a lot of people reckon he was the inspiration for James Bond. Also, it makes you wonder why they didn't change his first name as well – it's like when they put the Simpsons into the Witness Relocation Program and changed Homer's name to Homer Thompson because he would have been too thick to handle a different first name. Did MI5 do that just because William Melville was from Kerry? We can't rule it out.

Melville/Morgan was a celebrity good-guy in early twentieth-century London. His pursuit of anarchist bombers inspired Joseph Conrad's book *The Secret Agent*; his endorsement appeared on Harry Houdini posters (Houdini taught him how to pick locks); he also broke up a German spy ring in 1914. He was an action man as well, wrestling a French anarchist bomber to the ground in Victoria Station, who then tried to pull him under a train.

Sound like anyone you know? The next time someone says James Bond is the quintessential Englishman, remind them that he actually came from Sneem.

45

PEG PLUNKETT

Who?

You're not alone. Most men in eighteenth-century Dublin would have denied knowing anything about Peg Plunkett. Also known as Margaret Leeson, she was the most famous brothel madam in the city at the time – just reading about her life makes you feel like we live in boring times. (Yes, even now.)

Her original brothel, on Drogheda Street, was vandalised by a gang of wealthy thugs called 'The Pinking Dindies'. No, that isn't some autocorrect cock-up – there was a gang of rich ne'er-do-wells in the eighteenth century called The Pinking Dindies. Still, at least we don't tolerate boorish rich thugs in Ireland any more, which separates us from England, where you can (allegedly) shag a pig's head and still become prime minister.

Anyway, back to Peg, who was regarded as one of the brightest and most entertaining people around town in her time. She also made a habit of insulting royalty when she got a chance, which is never a bad thing. Peg retired from the brothel business after thirty years, only to discover that the IOUs she had been given by wealthy clients were worthless, so she ended up in debtor's prison. Her way out was to write a series of memoirs, because, as we all know, there is loads of money to be made from writing a few books. (Sorry, I fell out of my second-hand chair there with all the laughing.) Anyway, the books were a huge hit, particularly among people who hadn't frequented her brothel.

There are a few takeaways here. I can't think of anyone in English history that can match her gumption. And always pay your debts, particularly if it's to an Irish woman who has seen you with your pants down.

46

JOE BROLLY

Let's put him in here to represent those Irish people down the years who decided to howl at the moon and shag the consequences. Sinéad O'Connor, Mary Coughlan, Brendan Behan, Eamon Dunphy, Roy Keane, Davy Fitzgerald and Nell McCafferty – you don't have to agree with them to think they'd probably be good craic over a drink. (Behan is long dead, but he'd probably still have a pint with you.)

Brolly's done it all. An All-Ireland winner with Derry, a barrister, a writer, broadcaster, plays Chopin on the piano, a man who donated a kidney to a virtual stranger, but sometimes he can be a proper pain in the hole too, like the time he sat behind me at a wedding in Dublin and talked non-stop through the whole thing.

It was good chat though, the bit I could hear. He's a classic example of the First Rule of Irish Conversation – it doesn't matter what you say, just don't be a bore.

He once suggested that Kerry football had stopped producing winning footballers. When Kerry won in 2014, their star attacker Kieran Donaghy looked straight into the camera and said, 'What do you think of that, Joe Brolly?' Brolly shot back with: 'You'd know his father was from Tyrone.' It was short, sharp, funny and generous, a bit like the man himself.

Don't bother looking for an English equivalent; there isn't one. The best they can manage is probably Jeremy Clarkson. In this case, Maggie Thatcher, your boys took one hell of a beating.

47

WARRIOR QUEENS

Queen Maeve of Connacht spelled her name 'Medb'. This was unpronounceable for her greatest enemies, the Horse People of Mullingar, so they went to war with Queen Orla the Phonetic instead and wiped out her tribe, the Fish Folk of Tubbercurry. Even to this day, people around Sligo and Roscommon are reluctant to call their daughters Orla.

I made all that up. (Except for the spelling of Maeve/Medb.) It's the kind of bullshit you'd read on the side of a Brexit campaign bus. But we're talking ancient myths here, so it's whatever you're having yourself, really.

According to the Internet, Medb ruled the western province of Ireland, Connacht, during the first century AD. She was jealous that her husband had a great bull, so she tried to take one from Ulster, but her army was stopped by Cú Chulainn, at which point she stole the bull instead, and then she killed her husband (reason unclear) and renamed all her sons Maine. Furthermore, she was really into shagging and killing, until she was eventually killed herself in a lake when someone used a slingshot to hit her with a bit of old cheese (!!), after which she was buried standing up on top of Knocknarea Mountain in Sligo, so she could face her enemies in Ulster.

In contrast, England's Elizabeth I ruled for forty-four years, executed one cousin and died in her bed a virgin. I mean, come on – that's just a snoozefest compared to Medb.

48

MICHAEL COLLINS VS CHURCHILL

You can't really compare these two. One defeated one of the most evil aggressors in history against all the odds. The other was Winston Churchill. (Sorry, couldn't resist. Unlike Michael Collins, says you.)

It's not really Winston's fault that he'll never be a match for Michael Collins. For starters, he isn't from Cork. That's the equivalent of fighting with one arm tied behind your back.

Some say Churchill saved civilisation in its hour of greatest need. Others say he is the inspiration for Boris Johnson. This should be enough to destroy Churchill's legacy, even if, unlike Boris, Winston defeated fascism and knew how many kids he had.

The amazing thing about Churchill is that he seems to have achieved a lot of this while pissed off his head. Even more amazing is the 2015 article about his drinking in *The Daily Telegraph* that made the case that he wasn't an alcoholic. This is despite the fact that in 1936 he owed his wine merchant the equivalent of $75,000, had a type of champagne named after him and even had his own favourite breakfast wine, a German hock. Honestly, if there were a questionnaire to figure out if someone is an alcoholic, the first question would be 'Do you have a favourite breakfast wine?'

Bizarrely for an Irishman, Michael Collins seems to have been more interested in sex than he was in alcohol. There are reports about affairs with a number of women in England, along with recent claims that he was gay. Whatever the truth, it couldn't have hurt his reputation that he was known as 'The Big Fellow', says you, with a schoolboy snigger.

49

LOUIS WALSH

I'm sure there are people in England who think 'Louis Walsh' is the Irish term for revenge. After all, here is a man who took a look at the world of entertainment in 1993 and decided that it needed a bit of Boyzone. People have been up in front of the International War Crimes Court in the Hague for less, says you, like a right snob, because they sold twenty-five million records in the 1990s when you were in a shoe-gazing indie band called Hating Yourself.

Louis then gave us Westlife, who sold fifty million records worldwide (according to Wikipedia, but that doesn't make it wrong). But, more than anything, he's on this list for making *The X Factor* still just about watchable long after it switched from people butchering

Whitney Houston songs into a crying competition.

Let's face it, Simon Cowell seemed to give up on the whole thing somewhere around 2013 (he didn't even bother changing his T-shirt. The audience became cynical, realising it doesn't take much to turn someone into a pop star. (Louis had long since realised this, after his years working with Mikey Graham.) Something new was required to wow the viewers and Louis filled that gap with a series of hilarious hairstyles. (No one ever got fired for underestimating a Saturday night TV audience.)

On top of this, Louis gave us all a drinking game where you had to down a shot every time he said, 'You remind me of a young Ronan Keating.' As a result most of us were too shit-faced to notice that the show had gone completely down the jacks.

50

DARA Ó BRIAIN

Cheap Romanian wine arrived in Ireland in the mid-nineties. So did a lot of Romanian people, desperate to escape the hangovers that came from drinking their entry-level plonk. They must have been astounded when they saw us all tearing into their tractor-starter, but no one had given us wine for under a fiver before and we can be slow learners with alcohol.

I was halfway down such a bottle when I got to see Dara Ó Briain play one of his first gigs in a cafe in Ranelagh. Wine aside, I could see that he was funnier than a lot of what passed for comedy at the time. He has an amazing ability to say something nasty that comes across as funny – this is the exact opposite of loads of English comedians.

Unlike a lot of gag merchants, he can host anything from *Mock the Week* to *Robot Wars*. He has the common sense to understand that there is nothing funny about politics, doesn't pretend to be stupid and has even written a couple of books, the glory-hogging bastard. (One of these – *Tickling the English* – says nice things about our neighbours. Go on out of that Dara, ya big lick ya.)

This brings us to his biggest achievement: Dara Ó Briain has made a huge name for himself in London without half of Ireland deciding he is 'up himself'. That's as rare as dodging a hangover after a night on the Château du Bucharest.

51

MAURA HIGGINS' FANNY FLUTTERS

2019 was a tough year for England, what with no one liking them because of Brexit and Prince Andrew. What they needed was someone to come over from Ireland and give them fanny flutters. What they got was Maura Higgins and her 'fanny fluhers'. This was even better, because everything is twenty per cent funnier in a midlands accent.

It's hard for people from coastal areas to admit this, but midlanders are in fact more craic. (See the section on Shane Lowry if you need further persuasion.) The locals – anywhere from Laois to Cavan – are some of the most 'couldn't give a shite what you think' people in the world. Yes, there is a downside to the thinner gene pool away from the coast, but that's just a thing some of them have to take on their odd-shaped chins.

Maura Higgins doesn't have an odd-shaped chin. She's gorgeous and funny and reversed 400 years of Irish Catholic sex shame by talking about shagging and sex sweats for every waking hour while she was on *Love Island*. (If you look closely, you can actually see her saying 'fanny fluhers' in her sleep.)

She set the bar for reality TV. In her absence, the *Love Island* in early 2020 was as riveting as the afternoon session at an Ard-Fheis – people switched off in their thousands because twenty-somethings in swimwear are dead boring unless one of them is talking about sex sweats in a Longford accent.

SECTION 4

CULTURE

52

ANDREW SCOTT

I love Phoebe Waller-Bridge a bit too much for my wife's liking. I know people complain that she wouldn't have had the chance to create things like *Fleabag* and *Killing Eve* if she wasn't so posh. But come on, it's not her fault she was rich enough to get a meeting with the BBC.

But let's face it, for all of the Englishwoman's talent, *Fleabag* wouldn't have reached the heights it has without Ireland's Andrew Scott playing the hot priest in the final series. What an actor – fair play to him for playing a highly sexualised Irish priest without making every single Irish person run away and hide in the shed. ('Is he gone yet?' 'No, I think he's going to say his confession.' 'Jesus, that could take a while.')

Of course Scott was a legend before he brought *Fleabag* to the next level. You might remember him as the guy who lit up the screen as a bonkers supervillain, playing Moriarty in *Sherlock*. You could actually see Benedict Cumberbatch and Martin Freeman (Sherlock and Watson) looking at his performance and thinking, 'Ah, so that's how it's done.' (At least I could see it. And there's no such thing as truth any more, so my opinion is as good as any of your facts.)

By the way, Sir Arthur Conan Doyle, we spotted that you chose an Irish name like Moriarty for your villain in the Sherlock Holmes series. (We spot everything.) Aren't you the snaky boy now for doing that? What did we ever do to you?

53

THE IRISH LANGUAGE

It's amazing that the Irish language is still spoken around here. The English tried to belt it out of us. Then the nuns and the brothers tried to belt it back into us.

Yet it still persists. And not just because middle-class people send their kids to Gaelscoils so they don't have to mingle with immigrants. (It's not racist if you're making sure the teacher isn't distracted by kids who can't speak English, *an dtuigeann tú*?)

The fact is that the Irish language suits us. It's lyrical and funny and kind of unpredictable. Not only that, it only has eighteen letters in its alphabet. There's no j, k, v, x, y or z; those sounds are made up using a combination of other letters. I reckon we should push on until we get it down to one letter – maybe r – with the meaning determined by the look in your eye.

Anyway, it's ours and it's here to stay. If nothing else, for those moments when you hop in a cab with your friend in New York and say, '*Nach bhfuil an tiománaí tacsaí an-te?*' (Isn't the taxi driver very hot?) and the Puerto Rican driver turns around and says, '*Go raibh maith agat*', and you tell everyone and it goes mad viral. We fecking love that.

54

RIVERDANCE

The performance of Riverdance during the 1994 Eurovision has over 8 million views on YouTube.

A lot of us watched the original from behind the sofa. It was bad enough that we were hosting Eurovision again, torturing the people of Europe with a show full of songs aimed at tone-deaf Austrian teenagers who had terrible taste in clothes. But now we were going to make them sit through some Irish dancing at half-time?

Done properly, traditional dances involve people smiling a lot because they are just about to shag each other. Irish dancing, on the other hand, had usually involved people looking sad because they were not getting any. And then Riverdance came along and in fairness it was shagtastic. People were smiling and giving each other the eye, and that was just in the audience. (It didn't lead to anything – their 'rig-outs' were too off-putting.*)

England, on the other hand, has Morris dancing. Now, I don't know much about this Morris, but I doubt he was much of a dancer. In fairness, the dancers do seem to smile a lot, prancing around the maypole with straw coming out of their ears. I've no idea what they're so happy about, though – no one is going to shag them in those clogs.

* A rig-out is the outfit that was worn by Irish people at formal occasions in the mid-to-late twentieth century. They were designed by a crack team of nuns to rule out the slightest chance of any sex.

55

EUROVISION

Ireland 7 – UK 5. That's the good news in terms of Eurovision wins.

The bad news is one of those UK victories was in 1969 with a song called 'Boom Bang-a-Bang'. So it would be a mistake to take the competition too seriously. Except to note that song was sung by Lulu, who is from Scotland, so scores on the doors, Ireland 7 – England 4. (And that's before we get into the fact that Mike Nolan from Bucks Fizz was from Dublin, not to mention that Katrina from Katrina and the Waves came from the US.)

Anyway, you get the message. We're better than England at bad pop songs and let no one take that away from us. (The only way that's going to change is if people all across Europe decide to vote for something from England. If you reckon that's likely, you should probably spend more time watching the news.)

Ireland's success started with Dana in 1970, with 'All Kinds of Everything'. They put a wee postscript at the end of the title when she moved into politics – it read 'As Long as it Isn't Against the Teachings of the Church.'

Johnny Logan managed to win it twice during the 1980s, which we celebrated like mad because it was the only thing we won that whole decade outside of The Country Voted Most Likely to Move to America.

Finally it dawned on us that other countries were happy to give us their douze points because of the cost of hosting the shagging thing the next year. It's a little known fact that Linda Martin's winner in 1992, 'Why Me?', was written by the financial controller in RTÉ.

After years of trying to lose the thing, we ultimately sent a turkey called Dustin in a shopping trolley to the 2008 finals, hosted in Belgrade, insulting the hosts and large swathes of Europe. Thanks to their long memories, we probably won't win another Eurovision until 2125. But neither will England. What a result!

56

CHRIS O'DOWD

Roscommon deserves more. For too long now it has been the answer to the question, 'Where would be a good place to avoid tourists?' And, in fairness, when I googled Top 5 Tourist Attractions in Roscommon, one of them was a 'mining experience'.

But then you google 'famous people from Roscommon' and things become interesting. Top of the list is Emmy award-winner and all-round nice guy Chris O'Dowd. He broke big on TV in *The IT Crowd*, which showed that techy nerds could be adorable and even funny. I understand a group of people who married nerds off the back of that show are considering a class action lawsuit against the producers for false advertising, but these things happen.

The other breakout star from the show, England's Richard Ayoade, is also a walking, talking stick of human amazingness, which is a pain for me, because this book is supposed to show the Irish winning every time.

So here's a tiebreaker – which one of these actors went to Hollywood and out-hunked the guy from *Mad Men* in a movie called *Bridesmaids*? There you have it – another win for Ireland. And before any English reader accuses me of fixing the vote so someone from my crowd wins, I'd recommend you google 'constituency boundaries in the city of Derry'.

57

SHARON HORGAN

Sharon Horgan has a lot going for her. She's hilarious, empathetic, good-looking, a little vulnerable and you can pronounce her name phonetically. This last bit matters a lot if you're going to make it in the UK. It would have been more of a struggle if she was called Caoimhe, which sounds like the sort of name you'd give a rebel to make sure she avoids capture. 'What is the name of the Irish woman responsible for this, sergeant?' 'I can't pronounce it, sah!' 'Well then she must remain at large, free to attack the crown as she sees fit.'

Anyway, back to Sharon Horgan and her characters in *Pulling* and *Catastrophe*. Who knew that Irish women could be free-cursing pissheads with a relaxed attitude towards sex? Everyone, really. But she has managed to make them lovable and vulnerable as well, with an appeal that stretches from Sligo to Seattle.

I have a fair idea what you're going to say next. (I moonlight for a tech giant; we love listening in on your conversations.) Sharon Horgan is not as good as the aforementioned Phoebe Waller-Bridge, England. There's a one-word reply for that. Chris. You know Chris, the guy in *Catastrophe* played by Mark Bonnar (Scottish). Nobody has ever created a better comic character than Chris. So it's official. Sharon wins.

58

AISLING BEA

Sharon Horgan 2: This Time She's From Kildare. It's getting unfair on the English at this stage. Sharon Horgan used to be the absolute queen of TV giggles in the UK and then Aisling Bea wrote and starred (with Horgan) in the hit comedy *This Way Up*. It's more addictive than those Stollen Bites you get in Aldi every Christmas, you know, the ones with the marzipan hit in the middle. *This Way Up* is that good.

Her character, Áine, is gloriously pass-remarkable and very fond of self-medicating her mental health issues with a trip to the off-licence. Sound like anyone you know? Sound like everyone you know? She's as Irish as saying, 'I'll do that for you now, tomorrow.'

I can't really say she's better than Sharon Horgan,

because Sharon has a production company and, like everyone else in Ireland these days, I have a killer sitcom idea. (Sharon, call me.)

What I can say is that, at the time of writing, the Americans have started to notice Aisling Bea. She's done a comedy special and drama series, both of which you can watch on Netflix – if you can drag yourself away from hate-watching *The Crown*. I reckon it's only a matter of time before she becomes the funny version of James Corden. (There is only one thing to say about the *Gavin and Stacey Christmas Special* – you'd get more laughs from Radiohead.)

59

FATHER TED

The Catholic Church took all the fun out of life in Ireland, but *Father Ted* makes it all worthwhile (says no one who ever went to Mass here). It was all very well for the millions of Ted fans around the world – they never had to do the sign of peace handshake with Clammy Ciarán every Sunday and the small lake of sweat he used to store in the palm of his hand.

That said, *Father Ted* was hilarious. The closest the English could manage in response was *The Vicar of Dibley*. I could compare the two shows if you like, but who has the time for these things any more? We all lead such busy lives.

The show is commemorated every year with Tedfest, which seems like the opposite of a Ted Talk, in that the people who go there are keen to show off their low intelligence. I hear they spend a lot of time pretending to be that super-bore Fr Stone. People unfamiliar with going to Mass in Ireland probably think that he is a fictional character. Let me assure you, Fr Stone is Tommy Tiernan compared to some of the sermons we had to endure.

Still, this valley of tedium inspired Jack in *Father Ted*, played by the late and great Frank Kelly. When Dermot Morgan (Ted) died in 1998, a journalist asked Frank where he heard the news. The man who played the least priestly priest of all time said he heard about it when he got back from Mass. That is actually mad, Ted.

60

PIERCE BROSNAN

Can someone tell Daniel Craig that James Bond is supposed to be a joke? I know he's nearly done with the franchise now, but still, all he had to do was watch Roger Moore to see that the role cried out for a posh languid type with a thing for the ladies.

Instead he has to act all moody and grumpy, as if it's all downside when you're having sex with a beautiful woman on a super-yacht. It's amazing he never starred in a Bond movie called 'First World Problems Never Die Forever'. (What's with the cryptic titles anyway?)

Pierce Brosnan got that James Bond is a joke. (You don't have to be Irish to spot the hilarity of England still acting like a major player on the world stage, but it helps.)

He'd also be an absolute shoo-in if the Oscars had

a Lifetime Achievement Award for Getting Rid of a Navan Accent in the Interest of Your Career. (Anyone who thinks this is unfair hasn't had to wait around while a local pronounces the long 'a' in Naaaaaaaavan. You'd nearly be up to Dublin by the time they're finished.)

Brosnan was good at the acting bit as well, with plenty of standout moments in his four Bond movies. It was amazing the way he drove an invisible car in *Die Another Day*. Mind you, it must have helped that he came from poverty-stricken 1970s Ireland, where half the country owned an invisible car.

61

DERRY GIRLS

There's something about Derry. (Or Londonderry, for members of the Apprentice Boys who bought this book by mistake.)

Bronagh Gallagher, Feargal Sharkey, Nadine Coyle, John Hume, Seamus Heaney – the city and county always seems to punch above its weight. And now Derry has done it again with this hit TV show written by Lisa McGee. *Derry Girls* shows the resilience of people who get on with their lives in the face of some shocking atrocities, but enough about 1990s Irish fashion trends. (Or hair, says you, burning your debs photos out in the back garden before someone scans them onto Instagram.)

Now available on Netflix, the show has been getting

rave reviews from people all over the world, particularly from people who know how to work the subtitles. *Derry Girls* features standout performances from Jamie-Lee O'Donnell, Saoirse-Monica Jackson, Louisa Harland, Nicola Coughlan and Siobhán McSweeney. It even has Tommy Tiernan showing off his skills as a straight man. (Who knew?)

But spare a thought for Dylan Llewellyn, who plays the cousin over from the mainland. He's basically there so the others can fire cheap shots (by which I mean borderline hate-speech) at England and the English. You won't find any of that in this book, says you, keeping well away from our old friend the truth. And of course you won't find any TV show set in England that can match *Derry Girls* for charm and giggles. (Unless you have the mind of a seven-year-old boy and liked *The Inbetweeners*.)

62

MARIAN KEYES

Irish literary intellectuals are probably rolling their eyes at Marian's inclusion. Well, you know what, all four of ye can shag off. This Irish author has sold over forty million books worldwide and been translated into thirty-six languages.

But here's the thing – you don't have to read one of her bestsellers to appreciate genius at work. She deserves that title for the batshit hilarity of her Twitter account alone, where she has turned the phrase 'tanking you' into an ever-changing way of life. (The last time I checked it was 'tanken yew'; who knows what it is now.)

Marian has pulled off the old Irish writer stunt of doing things with the English language that seem to be beyond the people who invented it. She has also pulled off the old Irish writer stunt of doing all this while struggling with alcohol and depression.

Best of all, she's pulled it off and kept plenty of friends along the way. (Not something you might say about all Irish writers.) A growing fan base was able to enjoy her on the BBC Radio 4 series *Between Ourselves*, where she came across as a funny and grounded person without any notions about herself. (Another thing you can't say about many writers, Irish or otherwise.)

It's no surprise that she's popular across the water; they don't have an author/broadcaster/social media star who can compare.

I'm tempted to call her a National Treasure, but that's a horrible thing to say about anyone. Let's just say tanken yew, Marian, and leave it at that.

63

JEDWARD

I know, putting Jedward in the culture section is like giving Donald Trump a reward for services to the people of Mexico.

Jedward look like they were created in a lab by republicans as revenge against the English for the famine. (A sidebar for English readers who shunned history in favour of 'How come no one ever thanked us for invading their country?' in their GCSEs – the 1840s famine in Ireland killed one million people and forced another million to emigrate. Say what you will about the Irish, but we know how to suffer in round numbers.)

Anyway, where were we? Ah yes, Jedward. The boy-band where they were both the evil twin.

They appeared on *The X Factor* in 2009. Every week

they'd rush on and mock the notion that the show was somehow in the same category as Mozart, The Beatles or even Robson and Jerome.

Every week Simon Cowell would bury his head in his hairy hands at the prospect of another seven days of Jedward. Sensing their opportunity to upset a posh Englishman, every Irish person in the UK voted for Jedward, along with viewers under ten who loved their funny hair. As a result, Jedward lit up some lives and made it to week seven of the live show before they were knocked out by Olly Murs. That nearly hurt as much as the famine.

64

SAOIRSE RONAN

She was born in 1994. That's four Oscar nominations (three for best actress) before the age of thirty. She is going to be our very own Meryl Streep, our Olivia Colman with knobs on.

Saoirse has done all this with a name that is hard to pronounce, even for Irish people. Can you imagine the auditions she lost out on because the casting people were afraid they'd mess up her name? 'Let's call up Jennifer Lawrence instead. I love an actress with a lot of consonants.'

Born in the States to Irish parents, Saoirse grew up in Co. Carlow. She gets a fair bit of flak for not speaking in a Carlow accent. This is a completely unfair. There is no such thing as a Carlow accent; it's like they forgot to come up with their own and decided to just copy Kilkenny.

Her first best actress Oscar nomination was for *Brooklyn*, set in the 1950s, where her character Eilís can't decide between life in New York or Ireland. This is hilarious to anyone who lived in Ireland during the 1950s. (My father probably cursed four times in his entire life. I asked him one day what the 1950s were like. He said, 'Shit.')

A couple of hard-to-say-Irish-name tips for our English friends before we go.

1. Eilís is pronounced eye-leash.
2. Never ask an Irish person what Saoirse means, unless you fancy a four-hour Irish history lesson. I was going to say you could probably do with a four-hour history lesson, but my editor says I have to stop using that joke now, as it's starting to feel old. I said, 'You mean 800 years old?' He said, 'Just stop using the joke, okay?'

65

BATTLE OF THE ANTHEMS

The British national anthem is called 'God Save the Sad Rich Foreigners We Force to Live in Buckingham Palace and Pretend to Be Just Like Us'. Or the more current one, 'God Save The Queen from Her Own Family'. Of course it will shortly be solely known as the 'English national anthem', when the Celtic nations look at Brexit and say, 'These people are crazy, I'm out of here.'

Whatever the name, it's about as rousing as a song about fog.

Now, to be fair, the Irish national anthem wouldn't exactly have you goose-stepping either. It seems particularly tepid after you watch the French team furiously belting out 'La Marseillaise' before a rugby match against Ireland, where two words come to mind – oh shit.

The real strength of 'Amhrán na bhFiann' is that most of the people singing it have no idea what the words mean. This isn't just because they are in Irish – they're not exactly bursting with clarity when you translate them into English either. Unless you can see something I missed in 'Some have come from a land beyond the wave, Sworn to be free, no more our ancient sire land.' So when we sing our national anthem it's basically us just shouting a bunch of noises at the opposition. We might as well be doing the haka, without the sexy bits.

Compare that with 'God Save the Queen', with passages like 'Scatter our enemies, And make them fall, Confound their politics, Frustrate their knavish tricks.' That's all a bit Brexity, if you ask me.

66

BRENDA FRICKER

'When you're lying drunk at the airport, you're Irish. When you win an Oscar, you're British.'

Even if she never did another thing in her life, Brenda deserves her place in this book for that quote alone. (I haven't space to go into all the Irish people claimed by England here, because anyone who has more than a Junior B hurling medal on their CV has probably been claimed by London at some stage.)

But there is much more to Brenda Fricker than lethal quotes. For one thing, she won an Oscar for her part in *My Left Foot* in 1990. I don't know if she ever lay drunk in an airport, but if she didn't she's missing out, as it really is one of life's greatest pleasures. (Please drink responsibly.)

Full disclosure here. Her co-star in *My Left Foot* (who also won an Oscar) was England's Daniel Day-Lewis. We totally adopted him, though, along with half of Jack Charlton's football team, John Hurt, Chris Rea, David Gray and, a touch surprisingly, Joe Elliott from Def Leppard. But, in fairness, they all wanted to be adopted.

Back to Brenda before we go. Another career high was in *The Field*, where she appeared alongside Richard Harris, who attracted an Oscar nomination for his performance. I'd be amazed to hear that he wasn't claimed by certain sections of the London media after that nomination. And even more amazed to hear that he wasn't drunk in LA airport on his way home from the ceremony.

67

NOEL AND LIAM GALLAGHER

By the early 1990s we had done a lot of good work dismantling the stereotypical view of the All-Drinking, All-Cursing Paddy. (Prior to this, if someone pulled out of your talk show at the last minute, you could always get an Irish actor or George Best to come on and tell hilarious stories about their alcohol addiction.)

And then Oasis released *Definitely Maybe* in 1994, which put them on TV morning, noon and night with the big, boozy Mayo heads on them. I know they were born in Manchester, but it was to a woman called Peggy and it doesn't get much more Irish than that. It also looked like she cut their hair – again, very Irish there. And then of course there's the feud between the two of them that has been going on longer than a Martin Scorsese film. (The average length of an Irish grudge makes an Albanian blood feud look like something they'd resolve with a coin toss.)

But the most Irish thing of all is the compulsive cursing. It's not surprising that they told the world they were 'fooking mad' for it. The true mark of a Paddy (even second-generation ones) is someone who believes any sentence in the English language can be improved by adding the word 'fucking' to it. (Try it and see, guys; the results are fucking amazing. Hat tip to Scotland here too; love your work on this front.)

Long story short? Oasis are more Irish than English. And we're still fooking mad for them.

68

IRISH GOGGLEBOX

Before cable and satellite, there were two types of people in Ireland. Those who could get BBC and ITV with an aerial, and the rest of the country who hated their guts. It was just another example of divide and conquer from the Brits, says you, running for Sinn Féin at the next election.

The main reason we hated east-coast types is because the English make great telly, while, up until recently, quite a few shows on RTÉ were made by priests. (This isn't entirely untrue.)

In fairness, the UK *Gogglebox* carried on this tradition of amazing TV when it came out first, and not just because it was on at 9 p.m. on a Friday night and we were all on our second bottle of wine.

Unfortunately, after a couple of seasons, it lost the plot. The posh drunk couple were good value at the start, but you know the way it is with pissheads, you get sick of them after a while. Scarlett Moffatt ended up trying too hard, left the show and stopped being funny. The hairdresser guy in Brighton needs to get back with his ex. And there is no way Jenny and Lee are still in that caravan in Hull.

Meanwhile, the Irish *Gogglebox* has all of the giggles with none of the celebrity. If you think I'm wrong there, try to name one of the people on it. See? They've managed to keep their feet on the ground. (Up to now.)

69

MRS BROWN'S BOYS

6.8 million UK viewers watched *Mrs Brown's Boys* on Christmas Day 2017. The Queen's Christmas Message, on the other hand, got 5.9 million. This is amazing when you think about it – what possessed 5.9 million people to say, 'The turkey was a bit dry this year luv, so to make up for it I'm going to watch a member of the one per cent pretend to be just like me.'

Okay, look, it's not fair to compare Mrs Brown to the Queen. One is a woman with old-fashioned clothes and deadbeat kids – and the other one is Mrs Brown. Boom!

Still, for better or worse, Brendan O'Carroll's show has become part of the Christmas-Day tradition in the UK and Ireland, up there with prosecco for breakfast and third-degree burns because you sat next to the fire in your mother's place. (Christmas Day at home isn't hell – it's much hotter than that.)

The best thing about *Mrs Brown's Boys* is the snooty reviews it gets from people who think it's funny to shout 'Boris Johnson' at a pub full of students. *Mrs Brown's Boys* isn't a wry look at modern life or a savage satire on class and manners – it's two gags a minute and surprising levels of cursing for viewers who don't have an Irish mammy.

Say what you will about the English, but Mrs Brown, like Dame Edna, shows they have great time for a foreigner in a dress. (Unless it's Meghan Markle, of course. She stole their 'arry.)

70

COUNTRY AND IRISH

Some say that Country and Western music is the simplest form of popular music in the world. Others say you obviously never heard Country and Irish.

You won't find any fancy irony or reflection in Country and Irish music. Unless you've spotted hidden depths that I missed in songs like 'Friday at the Dance' or 'The Marquee in Drumlish'. The only big questions in these songs are 'When? and 'Where?' Some would add 'Why' to that list, but they are missing the point. Or maybe the pint. Because Country and Irish music is really about dancing, possibly after you've had a few drinks. (In fact, I wouldn't recommend listening to it without a few drinks.)

Don't worry about not knowing the song; they all

sound pretty much the same. They are usually about a mammy, a valley or a regular event where everyone has loads of craic. The lyrics rhyme, so, with a small bit of practice, you'll be able to guess what's coming next. As for dancing, just wear a slightly anxious smile and keep an eye on the person next to you. The songs have a Zen quality to them because they are completely free from anger. Even when Declan Nerney sings, 'Don't tell me what to do', he does it with a grand smile on his face.

England has given us Punk, Ska, Mod, New Wave, Dance and Britpop, and for that we are grateful. But sometimes you need a bit of simple pleasure in your life. And that's when you turn to Country and Irish.

71

ZIG AND ZAG

Go away with your Sooty and Basil Brush. The only scenario where the English could come up with a puppet to match Zig and Zag is one where Hitler managed to get Edward VIII back on the throne in the late 1930s. (Who would have thought a family whose real name is Saxe-Coburg-Gotha would have anything to do with the Germans?)

Zig and Zag's TV debut on *Dempsey's Den* in 1987 was the first sign that the people who made children's television in Ireland didn't actually hate children. Only ten years before that, Irish children were watching cartoons imported from the former Czechoslovakia. (Don't believe anyone who tells you that Czechoslovakia split in two in 1992 because of ethnic strife – it was all down to their shit cartoons.)

Suddenly you had two irreverent alien brothers who didn't seem like they were operated by a priest and a nun. Their relationship with Ian Dempsey and later Ray D'Arcy was like our relationship with our parents, just with less cursing.

Zig and Zag had a dizzy run of gigs after their move to the UK, including Channel 4's *Big Breakfast* in the 1990s, *Big Brother's Little Brother* in the noughties, and a show simply called *Zig and Zag* on CBBC. They also had a top five UK hit called 'Them Girls Them Girls', and they even met Donald Trump. There is no evidence that their song is based on that meeting, but you can never be sure with these things.

72

FLANN O'BRIEN

Real name Brian O'Nolan, aka Myles na gCopaleen. The greatest Irish writer of all time needed three names because he had three full-time jobs: the civil service, writing and downing balls of malt. (That's another name for a whiskey habit.)

A public servant couldn't write like Flann these days – he'd be too busy working, or enjoying one of his eighty-five days off a year says you bitterly to your cousin, the teacher.

His comedy masterpiece novels, such as *At Swim-Two-Birds* and *The Third Policeman*, made a very important point – reading is supposed to be enjoyable. Obviously if I say anything against James Joyce the paramilitary wing of the Irish intelligentsia will arrive at night and turn my children into swans – but still, the only people who can read Joyce without crying are the types who are very fond of the word 'wonderful'. (One thing you can say for certain about someone who says 'wonderful' is that they think you are beneath them.) As for Samuel Beckett, I know the point in some of his books is that nothing happens, but still, it would be nice if there was a bit of action now and again.

Flann O'Brien is your only man for a laugh. I was giggling so hard reading *The Dalkey Archive* on a tram in Frankfurt that I thought someone might report me to the authorities. And that book isn't even regarded as his best work.

He has no equal in the English language. And yes, I've heard of William Shakespeare and, like you, I never laughed at one of his jokes.

73

BONO

Look, at least he isn't Chris Martin.

It's weird. Here's a man who wrote all-time classics like 'One' and 'Stuck In a Moment You Can't Get Out Of'. He was one of the key drivers behind Band Aid and Live Aid. And still we feel like apologising to foreigners for him.

This would never have happened if himself and U2 didn't break America in 1987 with the release of *The Joshua Tree*. We loved America so much back then, half of the country lived in sweatshirts with USA on the front. The dream was to move there and make something of our lives. When U2 did just that, though, the begrudgery gnawed away at our souls.

Worse still, Bono and the band became really

positive and upbeat about things over the years. We hate that in Ireland. Or at least we used to. Despite our best efforts, there are worrying signs that younger generations see nothing wrong with feeling happy when one of their own does well. (What is wrong with these people?) On top of that most of them speak with an American accent.

So, if he can resist pushing another album into people's iPhones, there is every chance that Bono and U2 will finally be accepted in Ireland as some of the greatest musicians of their age.

It's about time. Yes, Bono can be a pain in the arse. But he's doing it for the right reasons. And more importantly, he's our pain in the arse.

And again, at least he's not Chris Martin.

74

THE PRESS

A pause in hostilities here to acknowledge the genius of the headline writers in English tabloids. There are plenty of contenders, but the gong goes to the sub-editor in 1984 who looked at a story that Frank Sinatra reportedly had sheep hormone injections to make him look younger and gave it the headline 'I've got Ewes Under My Skin'. Rumour has it that Piers Morgan was the sub-editor in question – I hope that hasn't ruined it for you.

Anyway, hostilities back on. So back to Piers Morgan, who was forced to apologise when, as editor of *The Mirror*, he splashed 'Achtung Surrender' before an England vs Germany game in 1996. That was seen as outlandish English nationalism back then – now it's the opening line of a Boris Johnson speech. In Berlin.

A lot of English tabloids have stopped being funny because there seems to be more money in thinly disguised racist comments against Muslims, continental Europeans, Leo Varadkar, Raheem Sterling and Americans who marry into the Royal Family.

Irish newspapers aren't blame free on this front. But very few of them feel like they are aimed at a guy called Lee in Sunderland, who is livid that he can't have the same job as his dad. And they can compete with the best of them when it comes to getting a laugh – unless you fail to see the funny side in the *Inish Times* headline 'Muff Annual Festival "A Must" For Black Mickey.'

The only thing funnier than the headline is the fact that you probably reckon that's a typo and I meant to write *Irish Times*. Really?

75

SHANE MacGOWAN

Okay, he was born in Kent, but even the British haven't tried to claim Shane MacGowan as one of their own. There's no way that face could come from any other country. (We'd have big ears what with all the cousin shagging.)

Starting out with a band called The Nipple Erectors (later The Nips), he was the only person on the London punk scene in the late 1970s who decided this isn't bad, but it could do with a few Irish rebel songs.

He edited a magazine called *Bondage* under the name of Shane O'Hooligan and got kicked out of Westminster Public School for smoking a joint. (And you thought you were cool for sneaking out at lunchtime to play pool.) He went on to meet Spider Stacy at a Ramones gig and soon we had The Pogues, one of the strangest marriages in rock 'n' roll.

The Pogues and MacGowan went on to make beautifully arranged, haunting songs like 'A Rainy Night in Soho', 'A Pair of Brown Eyes' and 'Sally MacLennane'. The people who made the best TV show of all time, *The Wire*, chose the Pogues' song 'Body of an American' for their iconic detective wake scenes. Have a look on You-Tube and you'll see why. It's a mad, boisterous celebration that somehow makes you want to cry.

But the best thing about Shane MacGowan? He makes this 101 Reasons list without even needing to mention 'The Fairytale of New York'. That's how good he is. And before you say England's Johnny Rotten was better, you might want to check your facts, because he's from Cork. (Kinda.)

76

SALLY ROONEY

It's incredible that her book *Normal People* won the award for International Author at the 2018 Specsavers National Book Awards in the UK. First of all, she was only twenty-seven. Secondly, the organisers didn't claim she was British. What's the world coming to?

Sally is in fact from Castlebar, and if she's related to Wayne Rooney, both of them are hiding it pretty well. Her debut novel, *Conversations with Friends*, earned her the title 'Salinger for the Snapchat Generation', which is a giant compliment, unless you're not too keen on twentieth-century American novelists. Her writing has appeared in *The New Yorker*, *The New York Times* and *The London Review of Books*. Lena Dunham loves her to bits and *Time* named her as one of the 100 most influential people in the world. Seriously, how come no one has claimed her as British? Someone should get fired for this.

If you think all Irish writers are delighted for Sally because she is one of our own, then you know nothing about Irish people or writers. We're weeping non-stop tears of jealous rage if you must know. Hey, we never claimed to be grown-up.

Unfortunately for us, but not the reading public, she isn't going away any time soon. Her own TV adaptation of *Normal People* on BBC is set to bring her to a whole new audience. After that it's just a matter of waiting for her next novel. And a *Daily Mail* article describing her as British (because it's bound to happen at some point).

77

THE YOUNG OFFENDERS

It's wrong to compare *Fleabag* with *The Young Offenders*. One is a nuanced take on life and love in one of the greatest cities in the world. The other is *Fleabag*. (I challenge you to find Cork and understatement in the same sentence – this one doesn't count.)

Heading into its third series with a growing audience, the show is built around bike chases and knob jokes. (Only a fool would try to make a comedy without those things after the success of *The Young Offenders*.) It is also built around Cork, the third biggest city on the island of Ireland for those of you from overseas or South County Dublin. (South County Dublin types know more about Barcelona than they do about life beyond the M50 – this is a true fact.)

Good news for Cork people – *The Young Offenders* will attract a lot of visitors to the city. Bad news – these visitors will have seen Cork on the show without realising it is shot during the twenty-seven minutes we get every year when it isn't pissing down with rain. (We call it summer.) So here are a few messages for English readers planning a trip to Cork. First of all, pass on my thanks to the Irish person who bought you this book as a joke, because nothing is funnier than a wildly inaccurate book aimed mainly at Irish-American tourists.

Secondly, do pay us a visit; it's great here in Cork and there's no chance of meeting anyone from Dublin. Also, check if someone with a name very like mine has written a book called *101 Reasons Why Cork is Better than Dublin*; I'm told it's an excellent guide to the city (by my mother).

Finally, bring an umbrella.

78

WINNING STREAK

Dear BBC executives, I have no intention of saying anything negative about your incredible institution. I would love to come on one of your highly rated TV shows to talk about my book. I'll even go on *Newsnight* and claim that *101 Reasons Why Ireland is Better than England* is an attempt to start a new conversation about the wonderfully complex relationship between our two nations, even though we both know it's a re-heat of some old Tayto jokes that I stole off Reddit.

If you would like me to go on *The Graham Norton Show*, I can be there in no time. In fact, if you look out the window, that's me in the van with blacked-out windows in the car park. I hope this doesn't come across as too stalkery; it's just that I'm a huge fan. (Hi, Graham.)

Anyway, back to the issue at hand. I pity the English – a lot of them have to make do with the BBC, along with ITV for game shows and Channel 4 for documentaries called *Fat, Poor and Thick* that mock people who didn't go to university. We get all of that, and RTÉ, along with Virgin Media and TG4, which is a media-training course for good-looking weather forecasters.

Some say that English people aren't missing anything because they don't have RTÉ. I've only two words for those people – *Winning Streak*. Enough of your skill-based game shows – *Countdown* is for nerds, *Catchphrase* is for idiots. The viewing public wants to veg on the couch on a Saturday night and watch people like themselves gambling on a giant slot machine. With *Winning Streak*, the public gets what the public wants. (Hat tip to The Jam's 'Going Underground' – every now and again, England is simply the best place in the world.)

SECTION 5

SPORT

79

THE PLOUGHING CHAMPIONSHIPS

Try telling the people who compete there that this isn't a sport.

Almost 300,000 people attended the 2019 ploughing championships in Co. Carlow. For overseas readers, 'The Ploughing', as it's known, is where country people gather in a giant field in their fifty-grand Land Rovers and complain about the decline of rural Ireland. (Only messing, some of them drive fifty-grand Mitsubishis.) The other main tribe is members of the Dublin media, huddled together in the Newstalk tent in case they meet an actual culchie. (For the uninitiated, the definition of 'a culchie' is someone who knows all the words to 'Wagon Wheel'. If you haven't heard that song before, you should try and keep it that way.)

The Ploughing is proof that Irish people will travel for hours just to look at each other in a field. England does have a ploughing championships, but I doubt that it attracts six per cent of the population.

The taoiseach (that's what we call our prime minister – you should hear what we call your prime minister) is obliged to be photographed there every year, handling a horse-drawn plough. You'd never see an English PM doing that, because the high level of mechanised farming there means a lot of the ploughing is done by robots. Although that should have been a good enough reason to invite Theresa May, says you.

80

THE GAA

The GAA is a sporting organisation that promotes belting the shite out of a guy from the neighbouring parish on a Sunday afternoon and then marrying his sister the following week. Only messing – he can marry the guy now if he likes, following the marriage equality referendum that legalised same-sex marriage in Ireland five years before England. (Who's backward now?)

There isn't much sexism in the GAA. Women are just as likely to belt the shite out of a woman from the neighbouring parish on a Sunday afternoon. The sports are played to a high level by people of all ages, genders and social classes – yes, posh people play it now because they love the cheap childcare in the summer. (They actually get horny at the mention of Cúl Camp.)

Despite its popularity, the stars don't make a cent out of playing, thus freeing up huge revenues that are then handed over to the Dublin GAA. (We all know it's true.)

The GAA is so strong that it can affect the quality of other elite sports on the island, though this still doesn't excuse the playing style of the Republic of Ireland senior men's football team. (They give you a free liver when you join the supporter's club – no one should be expected to watch that shite sober.)

GAA sports were never exported, so, unlike England, we never have to suffer the indignity of being shit at sports we invented. The lesson here is simple – if you don't want to lose to Burkina Faso at your national sport, then don't show them how to play it.

81

HURLING

Hurling is literally the stuff of legends, getting a mention in the epic Táin Bó Cúailnge, which dates back to the Iron Age in Ireland (500 BC to AD 400). The hero, Setanta, used a hurley and sliotar to kill a hound belonging to Cullen (Cú Chulainn in Gaelic). He then became Cullen's hound until a new dog could be trained to guard Cullen's home. So from then on Setanta was known as Cú Chulainn. I know, I think that's weird as well. The first rule of killing someone is don't change your name to theirs after the event – you're only drawing attention to yourself. Did Tony Soprano change his name to (spoiler alert) Big Pussy? No he did not.

Anyway, hurling was codified over time, where it changed from a bunch of guys hitting each other with sticks, to a bunch of guys hitting each other with sticks for seventy minutes plus injury time (aka, four hours). Seriously though, take a look at Joe Canning winning the 2017 All-Ireland semi-final for Galway with the last shot of the game from the sideline, fifty metres or more from goal, 68,000 people looking on, and you realise that this sport runs deep.

As deep as cricket does across England, I suppose, though that's where the similarity ends. For one thing, the Irish game is an amateur sport played by people representing their local area. And secondly, no one ever went to a hurling match just to catch up on some sleep.

82

FOOTBALL FANS

Irish football fans are only interested in one thing – making sure no one thinks they're English.

Sorry if that sounds nasty. The English people you meet abroad are almost always a delight. The problem is the English people who arrived before them down the centuries. I know, get over it and all that, but people don't like it when you take their farms. It's the one thing they'll tell their grandchildren.

Anyway, here's a tip for English fans when they travel overseas. There is a good chance your ancestors invaded the country you are visiting – so turning up as a knight in armour is a really bad look for you. Likewise, rampaging through the port area of a Mediterranean city and picking on Africans. The rest of the world hates that kind of stuff.

Nobody is saying Irish football fans are perfect. Mullingar Mick, in his tricolour drinking cape, is great craic until he spills a tray of the local BackenSlapper lager in your lap. But at least he's not throwing patio furniture at your local police.

So let's hear it for Mullingar Mick, even if he wears that manky tricolour cape every time he leaves the country. Yes, it looked plain wrong at that sales meeting in Zurich, but the important thing is that no one thought he was from England.

83

HORSE RACING

Good breeding doesn't always bring about the desired result – just look at some of the middle-rankers in the Royal Family. But the Irish seem to be very good at it when it comes to horses. A recent report found that twenty per cent of the top 100 flat horses in the world were Irish bred.

You could say it's something in our blood, as long as you don't suggest it might be something dodgy in the horses' blood, because we're talking horse racing here, not cycling or athletics. (Two things that the English are particularly good at – just saying.)

This probably goes back to the time when horse racing didn't have a whole lot to do with horses racing. Writing in the *Irish Examiner*, UCD historian Paul

Rouse examined the history of racing festivals in Ireland, quoting German writer Johann Georg Kohl and his 1844 book *Travels in Ireland*. According to Kohl, the racing was there as a supporting act for all sorts of carry-on, up to and including an actual 'Grinning Competition'. This isn't the best thing I've heard about Ireland – it's the best thing I've heard about anywhere.

This spirit is kept alive today at race meetings all over Ireland and further afield. They even have a modern take on the Grinning Competition, where the winner is the person who can't stop himself or herself from laughing when an Irish horse once again beats the English favourite at Cheltenham. We can be a small-minded, petty people when we put our minds to it …

84

ROY KEANE

If the robots really are coming for our jobs, the first gig on the line has to be football punditry. What's the point in advanced robotics and artificial intelligence if you can't teach a punditoid to say, 'For me, Gary, that's a penalty all day long.'

The only person they'll never replace is Roy Keane. Just as Sigmund Freud reportedly said that the Irish are impervious to psychoanalysis, Roy Keane is not something that can be recreated by an algorithm.

A lot of his analysis is, 'Ah come on Gary, you'd never get away with that in our time, man.' But that's gold compared to other pundits – it's as if broadcasters think we're happy to see former players read out stats at half-time. And yes, there is probably a market out there to watch millionaires tell you how many 'expected goals' Mo Salah had last season – but it's not as big as the market of people who want to see if Roy says something like, 'If Ashley Young is a Manchester United player, I'm a Chinaman.'

Now that's entertainment. (Unless you're Ashley Young.) It's simple enough really. Keane comes from a place that gave Eamon Dunphy and John Giles to the punditry world.

There was no way we'd ever allow someone like Alan Shearer on our screens. You see, you'd never get away with that at home, Gary.

85

MÍCHEÁL Ó MUIRCHEARTAIGH

Pronounced 'Me-hall O Mur-a-hurt-ig', for non-Irish readers, before you get a pain in your head. The only other sports commentator that can compare is the late Scottish rugby legend Bill McLaren. In fairness to Bill, he gave the world 'woof, what a boomer' long before that became the word for old people who are to blame for absolutely everything.

But he never came up with anything to compete with 'Teddy McCarthy to Mick McCarthy, no relation, Mick McCarthy back to Teddy McCarthy, still no relation.' That was Mícheál Ó Muircheartaigh on any given Sunday.

It would be an exaggeration to say he single-handedly

saved the Irish language from extinction, but I'm going to do it anyway. You see, I come from that generation that wanted revenge on the Irish language after it took the piss out of my teenage years. The only thing that gave me the slightest *grá* for Irish was listening to a match on RTÉ radio. You'd nearly be hoping someone would get injured so Mícheál could start freestyling (in English) about a dance in Castleisland, tickets on the door, €10, he was there himself last year on the way back from visiting a cousin in hospital in Tralee, she was in flying form and so was the dance. Next thing you know he's telling you Gooch Cooper's shot was '*go hard, go cruinn agus thar an dtrasnán*'. That's Irish for take that, ye Dublin gobshites.

Except of course it isn't. He might have bled Kerry, but he was always impartial. He remains one of the greatest commentators of all time. There's every chance he inspired you to get over your problem with the Irish language and send your kids to a Gaelscoil. Or maybe

you just liked the smaller class sizes – we can't rule that
out either.

86

PAUL O'CONNELL

There are two reasons Brian O'Driscoll isn't considered a legend all over Ireland. The first one is that he's associated with your average Leinster fan, Evan. The only thing you need to know about Evan is that no one likes him, not even his mother.

The other problem for 'Drico' is that he only has one nickname.

Paul O'Connell has two nicknames. Psycho is the first one – though I wouldn't use that to his face without checking that he was okay with it first. All we know is the name came from fellow Munster star Alan Quinlan, and if Alan Quinlan thinks you're a psycho, that's good enough for me.

The second nickname was conferred by his fellow

Irish players after they were knocked out of the Rugby World Cup in 2011. O'Connell went on a twenty-four-hour drinking session around Wellington, New Zealand. According to his autobiography, *The Battle*, a few hours into this session he bumped into Leinster player Fergus McFadden and a guy from Drogheda dressed as a leprechaun. They had a few drinks in the hotel bar; four hours later over breakfast and sparkling wine, O'Connell started giving out to the leprechaun because he was starting to fade, then the leprechaun ordered a round of whiskeys before heading home; three hours later O'Connell met up with his parents for a few beers; twelve hours later he went to bed. Apparently he wasn't looking great the following day, so from then on he was known by his second nickname: 'The Corpse'. It's all in the detail. I'm sure English rugby legends had some huge piss-ups. But I bet they never badgered a fading leprechaun into buying a round of whiskey.

87

CROKE PARK VS WEMBLEY

Croke Park is the showcase for GAA games in Ireland. The huge open terrace at the north end of the stadium is called Hill 16. This is where Dublin fans congregate and celebrate the fact that they have enough money to buy the All-Ireland Championship every year. (Only messing, they still haven't figured out how to do it in the hurling.)

For a long time, the GAA wouldn't allow football or rugby games in Croke Park. This was down to Rule 42, which stated: 'We'll have none of your English sports in here, unless we spend a fortune redeveloping the gaff and need the money.' As a result, Ireland played England in the Six Nations Rugby Championship there in 2007. We were so nervous of booing during 'God Save the

Queen' that the whole country went into a state of Pre-emptive Mortification.

Thankfully there were only a few boos heard around the stadium on the day, and that was from the English players who were forced by their rugby union to take the backlash for the whole 800 years of oppression thing. Ireland hammered them out the gate, 43–13.

It was fitting that one of the first non-GAA games there was against the old enemy. Two reasons for any English reader asking why: 1) Hill 16 is built in part with the rubble of O'Connell Street, which was largely destroyed during the 1916 Easter Rising, a rebellion when Irish rebels took control of strategic locations in Dublin city centre; and 2) Crown forces murdered fourteen innocent civilians there during a football game in 1920. There now, aren't you glad you asked?

Yes, Wembley has hosted Olympics, World Cups, and Live Aid. But it just doesn't have the Croke Park backstory.

88

GEORGE BEST

Pelé once described George Best as the greatest footballer of all time. This is accepted by people all over the world. Except of course in Cork, where Best isn't even regarded as the greatest Man United player of all time. Or even the second best – you need to see that free kick Denis Irwin scored against Liverpool in the 1993–94 campaign, langer.

A quick run-through of Best's best goals on YouTube will show you three things – the 1960s wasn't a great time for hairstyles, it was always foggy at night and George Best knew how to make football look beautiful. This wasn't easy when the guys trying to get the ball off you had names like Bites yer Legs or Chopper, sometimes on their birth certs, because their mothers just knew.

Best took a hacking in the 1968 European Cup when United beat Benfica in the final at Wembley. There's a video of him in that match on YouTube, where he appears to be from a different species to the other players on the pitch, a new type of being that was designed to play football while making eyes at women in the stand.

He was living proof that God doesn't exist – it's unfair to make someone that good at football look like an aphrodisiac. Of course, history would be much different if he'd been born in England. For one thing, they wouldn't have needed the help of a Russian linesman to win the World Cup. (We all know it's true.)

89

SHANE LOWRY

This is to take nothing away from Rory McIlroy, Pádraig Harrington or Graeme McDowell, who are outstanding in their own major-winning ways. But they still seem a bit golfy, if you know what I mean: serious in an American kind of way.

Shane Lowry isn't golfy. He always looks as if he's working on a prank. To see why he isn't like any other world-class golfer, just google 'Shane Lowry My Little Honda 50'. See what I mean – there he is in a Dublin pub soon after winning the 2019 British Open, singing a ditty about a workhorse motorbike with a giant grin. It is the opposite of golf.

Scroll down the page of videos and there is another one of him belting out 'The Fields of Athenry' in front of a crowded pub, using the Claret Jug trophy from the British Open to mark out the beat. You don't have to be a republican to see this as an act of revolution against golf club bores everywhere, but it helps.

The closest thing England has to this level of entertainment is Ian Poulter. He is that peculiar English thing, an eccentric, which means he wears funny-looking clothes. I don't know anything about Ian, but judging by other English eccentrics I've met, I hope I never end up sitting next to him on a bus. Which is the exact opposite of how I feel about Shane Lowry. (Not that he'd ever be seen dead on a bus. He drives a Honda 50.)

90

KATIE TAYLOR

The standout female boxer in the world. Olympic gold in 2012, five consecutive golds at the world championships, undefeated in professional bouts, one of seven boxers of either gender to hold all four major world titles at the same time. Oh yeah, and she once scored four goals for Ireland's U–19 women's team in a UEFA qualifier against Macedonia. She also played Gaelic football and camogie for local clubs near Bray, because she obviously has eighty-six hours in her day.

Ireland currently stands twenty-fourth in the table of Olympic boxing medals, behind a list of Eastern Europe countries that spent half the twentieth century eating steroids for their breakfast. We'd be lost without our boxing stars, given that we're not the best at running and jumping and taking performance-enhancing drugs, when everyone else is clearly mastering the art of 'marginal gains'. (I know, I know – the old asthma gets very bad coming up to a major event.)

Thanks to Katie Taylor, among others, Olympic boxing has Ireland in a tizzy once every four years. The whole country stops to watch when there's a medal at stake – there we are, praying to Jesus that the person next to us doesn't ask how the scoring works, because to be honest, we haven't a clue either.

The sport just isn't that big a deal for your average English person. Except for Boris Johnson – he's always keen to show off his boxers. (Not that he'd see himself as 'an average English person'.)

91

THE O'DONOVAN BROTHERS

Is The Boat Race:

A: A tussle between the two best crews in the world
  or
B: A trip down the Thames for posh boys from Oxford and Cambridge, watched by unspeakable types drinking Pimms?

I can see why you might choose A. After all, the 'The' in the title suggests that it's special. But then the English tend to put 'The' in a lot of things. The Open. The Grand National. The Queen. The RFU. The rest of the world (might as well not exist).

Rowing in Ireland is different. It's less about celebrating the posh people who rule over us and more about, em, rowing. And nothing says that louder than the O'Donovan brothers from Skibbereen.

Saying that, the world champion rowers and Olympic silver medallists also understand that rowing very fast isn't enough for your average spectator. (Mainly because they're not wrecked from Pimms and trying to catch the eye of Tiggy Von Posh-Twit.) So the O'Donovans make it entertaining with their post-race interviews. Outsiders might be surprised to hear that the boys are actually quite well spoken for people from Skibbereen. But the accent is only part of their charm. If they ever decide that they don't fancy the gig as world-class rowers, there is a career for them as world-class comedians. (Check out their appearance on *The Graham Norton Show* for confirmation.)

One thing is for certain – they're funnier than some pissed minor aristocrat in a stripy blazer lounging around Putney Bridge.

92

JAMES McCLEAN

You don't have to agree with James McClean to admire his courage. (I'm certainly not going to criticise his nationalism in a book that is basically called My Country is Better than Yours.)

The Irish international footballer and Derry man refuses to wear a poppy on his jersey during the annual commemoration across Britain because he feels it would disrespect the victims of Bloody Sunday in his home town of Derry. (Fourteen innocent people were shot dead by British forces there in 1972.)

The poppy is worn to remember those who died serving Britain during wartime. By refusing to wear it, McClean has put himself in the firing line for sectarian abuse. Luckily, football fans are calm and reasonable people who are willing to see the good in everyone, says no one who has ever been at a game. So McClean has been at the receiving end of death threats and abuse, some of it from supporters of his own team. He hasn't budged, calling out the bad stuff when it happens and making sure that clubs are forced to root out sectarian abuse.

McClean is no rabble-rouser, judging by a measured open letter he sent to a previous chairman, explaining that he would have no problem if the poppy just commemorated the dead of the First and Second World Wars.

He has taken a genuinely brave stance at a time when wearing the poppy is becoming increasingly politicised in England. People are going to extraordinary lengths to show their patriotic fervour every November by trying to out-poppy each other – it's only a matter of time before a BBC presenter appears with his head in a wreath of them. With nationalist tensions rising around the world,

McClean is doing the world a favour by reminding us that every war is a dirty business.

SECTION 6

FOOD & DRINK

93

TAYTO

Three words for anyone who thinks Ireland has never contributed anything to global cuisine – cheese and onion.

Joe Murphy didn't invent potato crisps, but the man who founded Tayto discovered that a cheese and onion flavour could take it to the next level. He originally offered three flavours – plain, cheese, and cheese and onion. It's safe to assume that anyone who went for cheese and onion in the early days got a name for being 'up themselves'. (Wasn't it well for them?)

This has changed and now Tayto is a byword for cheese and onion crisps. You'll find a couple of people who like salt and vinegar, but sure look there are perverts in every walk of life. Cheese and onion Tayto would be the snack of kings, if we were still dealing with a monarchy.

Meanwhile, in the monarchy next door, the poor English have fooled themselves into seeing nothing wrong with a potato snack that tastes like prawn cocktail. I'm no scientist, but that sounds like the kind of chemical messing that could interfere with the DNA of a potato and drive half the population around the twist. (Finally, an explanation for Brexit!)

Tayto has followed us around the world. The only reason it isn't top of a list called 'Things Emigrants Want When You Visit from Ireland' is because Solpadeine isn't available over the counter in the United States. There was a time there when Irish people were shipping more drugs through US customs than a medium-sized cartel. Netflix are currently making a six-part drama about it called *O'Narcos*. This isn't actually true, but it should be.

94

WHISKY

Calm down. This is not the wrong spelling for Irish whisky, or *whiskey* if you insist. According to the archivist at Irish Distillers (look at you getting a properly researched book for under seven quid), snobby nineteenth-century Dublin distilleries inserted the 'e' in the spelling to distinguish themselves from Belfast and Cork whisky, because that's the kind of thing that Dublin people do. But look, that's a subject for another book.

Anyway, the name stuck and the Irish version is normally spelt with an 'e'. (It's occasionally taken with an E, but that's another night out.)

The point is that no one ever said 'English' when asked what kind of whiskey they'd like. (Or at least they never said it twice.) According to the Internet, there is something called 'the English whisky movement', which I presume is the running motion you make when someone offers you a glass of the stuff.

The best thing about Irish whiskey is that it doesn't go off. So there is always a drop available when you get the slightest tickle in your throat and use it as an excuse to get smashed on hot toddies for the next three days. If you haven't heard of a hot toddy, the recipe is:

1. Phone work and tell them you're out until Monday week.
2. Add cloves, lemon and hot water to a double whisk(e)y.
3. Repeat until you start to lose the feeling in your legs.

95

BUTTER

If you don't remember THAT ad, search for 'Kerrygold Andre TV ad' on YouTube. There they all are in the kitchen when the French guy sidles up and says, 'There is something I can 'elp?' in an *'Allo 'Allo* accent that would get you done for a hate crime these days. The young Irish woman says, 'You could put a bit of butter on the spuds, Andre.' That's what Irish people said in the 1980s when they wanted you to have sex with them up against a wall.

No wonder some people reckon that Irish butter is pure sex. (Not that we'd have a problem with the impure stuff.)

We went off the butter for a while after that because consuming full-fat dairy meant you were in league with the devil. Anyway, science, which is never wrong, changed its mind completely about butter and now we're back pretty much spreading it on our limbs.

It's all in the grass, apparently. All that rain is good for something, and that something is the best-tasting butter in the world. It's so good that our ancient ancestors used to store it in peat. Over 270 examples of this have been dug up around Ireland – they call it 'bog butter'. This would be such a great name if it didn't sound like something you keep in the jacks to treat your piles.

But this doesn't take away from the fact that Irish butter is better than any other butter in the world. (Or at least English butter, which is all that matters to a lot of us.)

96

TRADITIONAL DISHES

Talking up Irish and English food is all right, I suppose – if you've never been to France. Or Italy. Or Thailand. Or, let's face it, the moon.

Food just isn't our thing. While other countries see food as something that will put them in touch with the angels, we're all about filling a gap.

But there's still no excuse for that English classic, Toad in the Hole. I don't care that it's a giant sausage roll – it sounds like a kick in the backside you'd get from a bouncer in Bognor Regis. ('Toed', in case you're wondering.)

The top English food is, of course, fish and chips. The brief was obviously 'design a meal for a nation that hates fish'. The solution is obviously 'coat it in two blocked arteries of batter, served with a heart attack of chips'.

I'm not saying Irish cuisine is blemish-free. It's hard to feel superior when you still have people eating skirts and kidneys of their own free will. (This is a stew made with pork offal that Irish people use in order to keep visitors away from their house. The smell is that bad.)

But England will never match an Irish stew. First up, you can just say, 'Irish Stew in the name of the law', and get a cheap laugh that way. ('I arrest you in the name of the law,' in case you're having one of those days.)

But it also wins hands down for tasting great and not giving you a heart attack. It's soupy and meaty and sweet and comforting, and they probably still wouldn't touch it in France during a famine. But at least it beats getting Toad in the Hole.

97

THE FULL IRISH

Let's get our definitions right first. I checked my life assurance policy there – if I have five Ulster fries in any ten-year period, the contract is invalid. I googled what's actually in the Ulster fry and my laptop had a heart attack. Anyway, enough of the music-hall jokes. The Ulster fry is a thing of beauty if you have four hours afterwards to deal with the meat and carb sweats.

The Full Irish breakfast is its little sister, without soda bread or potato bread. It is best enjoyed in a mid-range B&B with a mild hangover. Ideally the owner should have notions about going on *MasterChef*, so your sausage, rasher, black pudding, tomato and fried egg are done to perfection. Top tip – it isn't a Full Irish if she doesn't say 'now so' when she hands you the plate.

There is no point in having the Full Irish in a five-star spa resort hotel. It will be twice the price of the one in the mid-range B&B, won't be quite as nice and there will be something slightly off about the waitress saying 'now so' when she hands over the plate. (Only B&B owners are allowed to say that, it's pretty much in the Irish constitution.) Also never order the Full Irish in a greasy spoon – the fried egg will make it feel like you are eating a water-slide.

The only thing you will learn if you order one in England is that other countries are shite at making sausages. And that's all I have to say about the Full English. Now so.

98

PUDDING? REALLY?

The reason English people use the word 'pudding' instead of 'dessert' is down to their old friend the class system. Except not in the way you think. Pudding isn't the posh name for the sweet thing you have at the end of your meal; it's actually the lower-class one. Dessert is a bit too French, apparently. Now, I got that nugget straight off the Internet, so please don't repeat it if you end up as a contestant on *The Chase*.

But everything about pudding is enough to put you off your dessert.

Get a pudding haircut and no will want to have sex with you. (No wonder they were so popular with the monks.)

Rice pudding is basically a bowl of dog puke.

And the only reason anyone ever ate Christmas Pudding is because your mother went to the bother of making it and you don't want to see her cry on the big day.

Look up 'favourite English puddings' and you'll come across Spotted Dick. That sounds like the symptom of a sexually transmitted disease – how could anyone put that in their mouth? (Walk away. You're better than that.)

While I have you, scone has an 'e' at the end of it – what's with all the 'scon' shite?

You get none of this messing with your Irish desserts. They're delicious, and still come on a trolley in some places as a helpful reminder that you'll end up lying on one in a hospital corridor if you eat too much Black Forest gateau.

99

STOUT

Yes, I know stout started out in London before making its way across the Irish Sea. But given that Dublin is now the home of stout, the Londoners were obviously doing it all wrong.

They continue to do it all wrong. If you doubt this, then take a look at the Instagram account, shitlondonguinness. See what I mean? Big head, small head, no head, bubbles, and those are the good ones. It's nearly enough to put you off stout altogether.

The issue here is one of respect. English people don't take drinking seriously, which is why they tend to use comedy names for their pubs and beer. As I said at the start of the book, anyone drinking a pint of Village Idiot in The Bishop's G-String is missing the point –

drinking is a serious business.

That's why our beers and pubs are named after people, instead of a line from a Monty Python sketch. It's not unusual to order a pint of Guinness in a pub called O'Hanlon's and ask Mrs O'Hanlon herself to fix it if it has a wonky head.

(Quick digression. I want to be able to walk down the street in my hometown of Cork without being called a Dublin-loving langer, so I should add that Guinness isn't the only stout in Ireland and, in fact, Beamish and Murphy's are at least as good. Just said I'd get that out there.)

Anyway, our seriousness about stout is why Guinness is a byword for a good bevvy all over the world, while English beer is more of a punchline. In fact, the queue for a taxi outside The Bishop's G-String is literally a punch line – English people get fierce fighty after a few pints of Village Idiot.

100

SPUD LOVE

Let's hear it for the humble spud, *solanum tuberosum*. (I've started dropping Latin into my everyday conversation to fool people about my unusually low IQ. Look, if it can work for Boris Johnson …)

And yes, I know that England's Walter Raleigh introduced potatoes here in the sixteenth century, when he planted them on his estate in Co. Cork. But it's fair to say that we picked it up and ran with it on the spud front from there on. This is because the potato is a hardy lad that will grow on a barren moonscape – or the west coast of Ireland as it's known locally.

The high point of our potato madness comes around every December. You are basically in league with the devil if your Christmas dinner table doesn't include roasties, mash, potato croquettes, potato stuffing, potato gratin and a bowl of Tayto. (Don't be surprised if someone throws a wobbler because there are no baked potatoes.)

This spud frenzy is no bad thing. They're full of vitamins and fibre, and low in cholesterol – as long as you don't add a half pound of butter, which you do because you're Irish and isn't it the way you were brought up. Whatever way you like it, we're lucky to have potatoes in our lives.

I know the English like them as well, but our spud love takes it to the next level. Put it this way – imagine what we'd think of potatoes if they hadn't let us down in a famine that resulted in a million deaths?

101

PUB GRUB

There's one problem with the English pub-grub classic, the ploughman's lunch. It's in the name: 'Ploughman'? Seriously, I've never seen anything to suggest that they are top foodies and we should follow their every move on the lunch front. Would it not have been a better idea to go with something like 'Chef's Lunch'? Yes it would.

I know England has moved on. They have gastro pubs these days, where the ploughman's menu description includes the words 'artisan', 'small batches', 'local', 'handmade', 'passion' and as a result it now costs you £14.99. Now that's what I call progress.

Things have moved on in Ireland too, from the time when you were considered a bit up yourself if you went for a second purple Snack. But you are still never more than ten metres away from our old friend, the toasted special. No one ever orders a toasted special – it's always 'The Toasted Special Without Tomato.' (A tomato in a toasted sandwich is about as appetising as half an hour with Katie Hopkins.)

The toasted special without tomato remains one of the great culinary treats in Ireland, particularly if you like your lunch served with ten slightly stale Hunky Dories, or a scrap of side-salad if you are dining in Dublin 4.

The toasted special isn't the only option on the menu – you could always go for 'The Soup'. This involves the following conversation:

You: 'What's the soup today?'
Waiter: 'Vegetable.'
You: 'Has it ever been anything other than vegetable?'
Waiter: 'No. A bar owner in Roscommon tried cream of mushroom one day, but he lost all his customers.'

ACKNOWLEDGEMENTS

First up, thanks to my amazing, funny, hot wife, Rose, for letting me give up an actual money-paying job to become a writer. Seriously, what were you thinking?!! Thanks to our kids, Freda and Joe, for all the dancing and stories about sand sharks – it was a great distraction amid endless hours of writing about Boris Johnson and the famine.

Thanks also to the crew at the publishers, Mercier, who gave me loads of latitude writing this, and then a little tug back when I might have gone too far. Deirdre, Noel, Wendy, Alice, I'd be lost without ye.